DIMENSIONS

POEMS, VIGNETTES, AND FLASH FICTION

JEREMY GRAVILORE

OCEANNAPOLIS

Dedicated to a bright future for mankind

Contents

PREFACE

Cultural change accelerated in 2020. Life endured shutdowns and ideological animosities. During traumatic transformations, people suffered, adapted, and rediscovered inner strengths and weaknesses.

Troubles continue in 2024. People seek what they lost... and what they never had. They turn to the questions that fill them with awe and doubt. Society grapples with eternal themes that spotlight frailties and showcase fortitude.

Drops of initial doubt turn into wellsprings of faith. Demons release the hounds of hell to persecute, and angels deliver miracles to persevere. We find refuge in our Creator's warnings and marvels.

Welcome to *Dimensions*.

Jeremy Gravilore, February 2024

JOURNEYS (POEMS I)

Age of Psychosis

Free the animals!

No aquariums

No zoos

No cages

Cage the humans!

Join the collective

Stay in line

Conform

Lobster's Shadow

The lobster stares at his reflection in the glass tank

Majestic crustacean

Claws banded

Solitude amongst the fish

No predators, no prey

Just stares at his reflection in the glass tank

Cycles until the End of Time

Oceanic symphonies arrange the orchestra of sight and sound that no earthly composer can rival

The sky and clouds join the procession before conducting a separate opus

Guest starring the musicians of land, with hallowed instruments all their own

The End

A grand civilization crashes to its death

Escape pods melt in the cultural inferno

The monsters dance upon the remnants of society

Living demons swallow the last vestiges of hope

Toward Becoming a Man

A human with his face, eyes, mouth, ears, nose

A creature with his claws, fangs, tail, and horns

The same man embodies the human and the creature

Who will prevail?

Another Drink

A beautiful bay scape

Overtaken by the air of the séance

Happy hour soothes the willing and able participants

The angels weep

The Ghost Watchman

Disappear

Detect

Rest

Haunt

Friends?

Good times

Good people

A great deceit

Forged in longing

Using

Injuring

Envy

Now detached

Brotherhood of Phony Friends

Brotherhood of rum

Brotherhood of loneliness

Brotherhood of boredom

Brotherhood of weakness

The Great Horror

Societal virus

Lockdowns and muzzles shroud the land

Empty faces pounce with anger

Sycophants cast judgments from on high

The high of their own self-perceptions as the virtuous

Murderous pride casts its fiery net

Intractable Isolation

Liars, pimps, whores, and thieves hold court and deliver their ruling

Stay home, lifeless

No travel

Nor adventure

Nor vigor

Back to normal, void of heartiness and cheer

The era of the do-gooder liar, pimp, whore, and thief has arrived

A Summer Worth Living

Swam in the ocean

Washed out

Walked into sunset

Ate clams

Watched the clouds

Argued

Lost relationships

All of this, and somehow the galaxy survived

The Solitary Duck

The duck glides slowly along the glistening river

Watching the people embark on a boat as the sun shines across
the valley

Born a ship without need for alteration, the duck navigates the
waterway flawlessly

Dolphins and whales swim the open seas

The duck is content with the river, traversing the land

Sightseeing man-made structures that the most ambitious

oceanic mammal will never experience

The Most Beautiful Drive

Sweeping view of the coast

Forested hills gaze over the vast expanse of blue

Cloudless day offers a cloudless mind to explore nature and spirit

Not one bad omen in the sky

The promise of summer lives and thrives from the high overlook down to the grain of sand

Twenty Years

Peering through the trees outside my old rental to the mountains in the distance

The mountains offer the pledge of future treks through the unknown

Turbulence and nightmares, but also peace and sweet dreams

One with nature, yet one with mind, body, and spirit

Twenty years later

The unknown lurks in the mountains, the plateaus, the sea, and the suburbs

From coast to coast and all terrain in between

Confident Cliffs

Waves crash into the cliffs

Changing tides of civilization

A decade brings gargantuan shifts to society

A decade brings no discernable alterations to the cycle of waves
or the cliffs they smack

Cattle Crossing

A hot desert wind picks up across the floor of the canyon

Vegetation thirsting for nothing other than what its surround-
ings provide

The adaptable trees and shrubs stare at the "Open Range" sign

Cattle have ongoing visitation rights to roam the endless moun-
tains and horizon of the Southwest

First Visit

First visit to South Carolina

The beautiful Atlantic waters welcomed me in late March

A peaceful seaside oasis with the opaque spirits of alligators

Boats strolled along the sea and along the neighborhood docks

Spring break for some

Golfing for others

The first auto voyage on the East Coast in over ten years

A realization the original thirteen colonies became my home once again

Time Decay

It was 2012

A young man, with faint and ignorable angels and demons of the afterworld

Surrounded by family and friends, a celebration back where it all began in the Garden state

The palpable memories of the West faded, though never forgotten

Old companions, some new ones, and a whirlwind of still

youthful years on the way

The angels and demons would become louder, warning of rapid
time decay

After a few blinks, 111 months, eclipses, blood moons, and
shifting ground

Young, but with the ever-growing awareness of heaven and hell
in the afterlife

And heaven in every waking hour

The City that Could Never Be

The fog rolls over the buildings as the boat sets off from the pier

Off to the islands in the Sound

The cool air whips our flapping jackets aboard the vessel

No cares could sabotage this open-water excursion

Just visiting now

Magnificent pastimes, and some bad ones

The city and greater region rejected our desires to grow roots

Cloudy skies welcome us back to the city's mainland, where we
continued

To capture experiences to take back to the places we call home

The Heist

My ex-bride's face disappears before me

The day meant to forge an impenetrable bond

Seeds of hatred sprout into weeds that suffocate the promise

My soul roaming for countless sunrises and sunsets

Not to find her

But to find the missing pieces of what she stole

Recapture

The time has arrived

I reclaim my spirit from the devils that stripped it away

No more cheapening the name my ancestors passed down

At long last, I see the universal light beaming all around

What Summer?

A cool early evening along the water

Early August feels like early October

Vacations in full swing with muted joy

Subtle eeriness fills the air, dispiriting the normal summer happiness along the decrepit boardwalk

Ocean Home

Many places to travel

Many places across the nation

Solace among the mountains, rivers, lakes, bays, and forests

Only the sea provides a knowing that I am in the right place

The ocean is my home

And it always will be

The Lone Black Bear

Quiet skies

The valley serves fresh air through the countryside

The side road disappears in a panoramic stretch of land that slows time

A solitary black bear stands tall in the serenity

The moment turns into a peaceful still frame for the human onlookers

My memory continues replaying a dynamic movie of the bear's
natural mountain home

The silent arena turns back to road as the humans move along

The lone black bear remains in the solitude of a place so real

Imagination and technical ingenuity could never reproduce the
setting

Tennessee August

It's good being back in the highlands

Villages appear through the mist

Tree-lined roads saturate the Blue Ridge

Summer magnetizes the majestic mountains

The majestic mountains magnetize the summer

Tennessee brings new August memories through the mist of the
past

The Forested River

Water glides over the rocks and stones
Trees take naps as torrents and gravity shuttle the occasional
branches along the banks

Life flourishes in the river and on the periphery

The ecosystem creates music, with no guitars, drums, or bassline vibrations

En route to Durango

A rock formation stands guard in the desert southwest

Many years west of the Colorado, with this first voyage to Durango

Many unforeseen adventures yet to be

The travel continues as the rock formation bids farewell

Sal

A man died last night in his sleep

I met him years ago, only once or twice

Friend of a friend

When he met me, he was sincere in a way rarely witnessed

Decent, genuine, and mature at 20 years old

Time is so short

Though I haven't seen Sal since last century, he made a greater impression on me than many I know well

The universe is a better place for Sal having been in it

From Death to Life

And someday we will die

Seeing all the faces of those that gave us indelible life memories, whose imprints on the afterlife we surmise

Loved ones cannot and should not join us on our own journeys across the threshold

Into the hereafter we all will sail, separately

What new beginnings await our spirits after passing?

The sorrows and laughter reverberate across the universe

We leave the emotions behind

To hear their faint sounds and the soulful knocking across the portals

Portals of our mothers, fathers, brothers, sisters, sons, and daughters

The love continues to propagate from death to afterlife

October, You're almost Perfect

It's a beautiful time of year

A lot of wonderful memories

The sky offers future memories for October and all seasons

But no matter what, I'm always yearning for summer

The Accidental Journey

Warm June day in the cool Northwest

The sea awaits you below the green-covered cliffs

What life beckons where salt water meets ground?

Beyond time and schedule, a galaxy of sea creatures whispers for your visit

You follow the calling and the mental photographs swim back and forth in your mind twelve years later

Future accidental journeys await, all part of your purposeful quest

What More?

What exists beyond food and water, shelter and health, family and friends?

A toast to the New Year, with little reconciled from the past months

Looking to the future, with a garbled understanding of the present

A bevy of fortunes, without wisdom for growing them

Dinosaur?

What meaning disappears as the physical world slides into oblivion?

Communicating on platforms with distant acquaintances and frenemies we love to hate and hate to love

Constantly judging every move made by those we claim to appreciate

Communities with little to no warmth, clinging to surface level bonds of affection

Can the dinosaur live and thrive among the modern, when the meteors of superficiality bombard the remnants?

The remnants of connecting become extinct

Alas, the dinosaur cannot survive

Yet those who appreciate the dinosaur can excel in the post-apocalyptic world of disjointed realities

The prehistoric and historic will live on and carry forth old-time meaning to the successors of bygone eras

Desolation

A housing complex, surrounded by housing complexes, surrounded by stores

No charm in a town of zombies and frost, even in the sizzling summer sun

Cliques of provincial demigods, confident and emboldened by the power they hold

A power over their tiny spaces of nothingness

In the near distance, the once-great cities provide a stream of refugees that somehow add to suburban desolation

The time freeze of March 2020 continues unabated

Glimpses of normalcy fade more quickly than they appear

Tree-cleared land makes way for a new housing complex of a salivating homeowners association

The weather turns cold, and the town turns colder

Demon Followers

No one goes anywhere

No one does anything

A never-ending state of fear cloaks entire regions

Madness descended and paralyzed the hustle and bustle

The demons toast to the death of vibrancy

Follow or perish

Compel others to follow

Let your heart ingest hatred for all remnants of individuality

Scour

Masked zombies trudge along the aisles at the grocery store

Expressionless, possessed, fearful

Ready to conform to the will of their cultural masters

Items become scarcer by the week

What if destitution overcomes the town?

When will one family fight the next?

How much time before the people become emptier than the shelves they scour?

They already have

The Cape of Pretentious Balance

The royal moderate preaches understanding

Speaks calmly

Asks for an open mind

Wants all sides to have their say

Then, the cape of politeness and formalities unravels

The royal moderate shows little regard for profound understanding

His anger rises to the cracked surface as the fault lines unsheathe a molten river of wanton hatred

He has no vision in his constipated mind

He stands on his own shoulders and blares trumpets in honor of his self-perceived inner beauty

The moderate was not so moderate after all

Sacrifice to the Goddess

And so I reflect as I walk the solitary land

Waves seesaw in the dead of winter, with the voices of summer long evaporated from the sandy beach

Friends of the recent past spring to mind

Weak friends, who would sell you out for three magic beans, a cow, or the illusory love of a propped up Venus

A friend offers tribute to his wife

Not riches from across the land

Rather, his identity for her to suck all the vigor out of his body

While she drugs him full of servitude to her splendor

The friend prays before the altar of his goddess, with me as one of his sacrifices to appease the goddess

The deity showers down lightning to vaporize my existence from the servant's life

I disappear from the altar the servant constructed as the immortal divinity consumes me

Venus obliterates my existence with the willing hand of the evil sorcerer, who used to call himself my friend

After all the storms and sacrifices, who remains?

The Venus inundates my former friend with lightning to devour him

My old companion pleads for mercy and remembers my friendship

His remaining happiness burns on the altar

The Floridian Ripening

Bright futures await the people seeking Florida

Much more than a land, Florida represents an idea

A zone of great fortunes and opportunities stretching across the mind's topography

The American Zion

Perhaps not a land of milk and honey

But a constellation of sweeping orange groves, bordered by a vast sea of marlins

The fruitful sunrise casts its light upon all the worthy beings

Man, iguana, dolphin, and gator rejoice

Go southeast, young man

Go southeast

All the Galaxy Is a Stage

Celestial curtains open

The nightly show commences

Comets stream across the sky

Meteors hurl toward deep black space

Stars shine across time as human observers gaze into the past

Lone planets envy the life-infused blue planet

The moon continues its gravitational assertions to remind the Earthlings of lunar significance

The sunlight switches back on

And the heavens become invisible until the nightly actors step back onto the cosmological stage

Wings of Hope

Best friends absent

Fled like Homo sapiens from an alien invasion

You stand alone among man

But the angels fly you past the betrayal and desolation woven by your corrupted spirit and demonic compadres

Dying Figments

Lost in a sea of writhing thought

A calmness pervades the waves of confusion

Peace of mind multiplies within the waters of the spirit

Imaginary monsters drown in your mind as tsunamis of panic collapse

Sanibel and Captiva

Aquatic zones of rest and vibrancy across the Gulf littorals

The islands provide sanctuary in this natural palace of the American tropics

The moonrise follows the sunset as the Ides of March pass once again

Crossing back to the Florida mainland

Craving a speedy return to the magical isles of sunshine and freedom

Birthday Gathering

Neither party nor feast

A get together of several people

At least one does not want to be there

He feels the weight of his wife's voice

The days of friendships have passed into a time of automatons keeping in touch out of robotic necessity

Familiarity overtaken by contempt for any burden to spend more than an hour's time in prior company

The sun sets on old friendships

The sun rises as the bonds of meaningless affections evaporate

Brilliant Light

Majestic luminescence awakens the consciousness of all willing souls

Creatures and vegetation glow in the radiance flowing across space time

Light promises a hopeful future as every photon fills the empty void

Eternal brightness permeates and energizes the spirits of the faithful

Arrhythmic

Once upon a time, society's heartbeat found the rhythm of a metronome

Now, the heartbeat flails out of tempo

Damaged ventricles no longer act as surefire conduits

Conduits that would carry essential nutrients throughout the cultural body

Individuals follow suit, off kilter and embracing hopelessness as past optimism yields a scant harvest

Society needs a special defibrillator stat

But the surgeons cannot find one amidst shortages in the cultural supply chain

Over and out

She offers a warmth that generates his continued longing for her

Later turns colder than absolute zero

Then becomes dismissive, ignoring him to stir up his longing for both her warmth and frost

The cycle of an aborted relationship within one week

No true rhyme or reason

She shared passions and pains

Engaged in profound conversation

It was merely the wisp of a dream

Stranded forever in the night sky they once gazed at together in a moment of fleeting harmony

Stormy Weather

Storms raged across the sky as they did across Roger's heart

He sat peacefully, waiting out the rain-soaked convoy of clouds

It seemed the rain sought to drench Roger, but he knew otherwise

Patient in waiting under shelter and watching the torrents pass

Thunder boomed

Lightning flashed

Roger knew they were mere sounds and sights

As the storm cleared, a solar beam and a soft breeze appeared

Roger ventured into the elements with a mostly sunny heart

The Real Outcast

The real outcast is neither friend nor foe

Neither family nor stranger

Neither rebel nor conformist

Belongs to nobody, and nobody belongs to him

The real outcast seeks neither cheers nor boos

Receives neither cheers nor boos

Basks in neither cheers nor boos

The real outcast is neither you nor I

The real outcast is the soul who quietly endures our arrows of gossip and rips apart our bow of animosity

Senses Gone

The people grasp at illusory connections

Smiles fade as the sun always sets

Agitated men watch the clocks tick quickly as the days drag on

The months bring fresh surprises of drudgery to the depressed seekers of shade and shadow

Traveling the Same Ground

At land and at sea, the days and locations repeat

A long cycle of similar faces

An endless cycle of the same personalities

Nobody new

No place new

Just the same people inhabiting the same area at the same time

Thus is the state of the traveler

Seeking new ground but finding trampled memories across the landscape of a new normal

Summer in Gettysburg

Henry entered Pennsylvania in the late afternoon on Independence Day

He crossed the state border into the old North

The gentle ghosts of past battles accompanied Henry on his travels throughout Gettysburg

They called on him to traverse the beautiful fields

And adopt the lessons of the memorialized fight between brothers

The horrors of nineteenth century civil strife interspersed with
Henry's favorite summertime memories

Ice cream shops, pubs, tours, and scenic buildings lined the
Main Street

Gettysburg, with a loud quiet stretching over cemeteries of
buried animosities and buried bones of the war dead

Henry visited the headstones and reflected on the lost

The Civil War did not create a permanent national harmony

Rather, independence marked the first step in liberty's contin-
ued march beyond the fields of the Union victory

Henry took a break from the historical tumult

Ordered ice cream and found himself firmly in the present on a
carefree summer's day

He could never thank the war dead enough

Fortunately for Henry, Gettysburg and its old and modern
character have not perished from the Earth

Solo: Traveling Across Time and Space

Welcome to the galaxy of the solo traveler

East to West

North to South

Backwards and Forwards

Up and Down

Trails, roads, water, and sky

Hiking boots, gas pedal, starboard deck, economy class

Time and space oscillate between contraction and expansion

Time and the cosmos guide the solo traveler

But his spirit brings him from regions dimmer than the oceanic depths

To luminosity beyond the brightest celestial bodies

SILHOUETTES (POEMS II)

Supernova: Chasing Light in a Time of Horror

Where does the light travel as decrepit gods stamp out illumination?

Radiant beams dissipate and reconstitute as the angels try to baptize zombies back to human form

The nightmare continues in slow motion

An explosion of vibrancy cannot thrust the zombies back to life

You lie within reach of the supernova

The blast dissolves you

Charlatans

Know-it-all bastards

Playing it cool and acting as though they are above the fray

Yet they jump in at moments of their choosing

Showcasing knowledge that lacks relevance to current or future circumstances

Social media made them more pointless than they could ever conceive

Safe in their self-described moderation, one can see through their anger and frustration

Their issues are theirs to consume you

Their voices drown in a sea of their own clichés and cliques

Charlatans and their misapplied knowledge amount to nothing

I hope they enjoy the void

Moonrise Cinema

The moon rises over the Gulf of Mexico

Stars glimmer, overshadowed by the lunar luminosity

The moon's performance achieves its stellar accolades because of the executive producer

It is the sun that arranged the lighting for the moon's nearside
face

Lunar stillness reigns through the night under an ongoing,
off-Broadway solar production

Mileage

Human vehicle still in service

After traveling long distances

Engine light comes on for tune-ups

Injured arm

Fractured toe

Tweaked back

Further long-distance travels on the way

Time for repairs

In the Window

Simpler times bred simpler machines

Summer heat overtook the house

No central air, hot or cold

Loud AC units for the windowsills

Installed in late May and removed in late September

Running into the house from the heat

Bringing your face right up to the vents

Cold air easing the sweat pouring from your face

Back outside for Wiffle ball

Hot and muggy sky would force you once again to refresh yourself right up close to the loud AC currents

Crackling Skies

A summer storm plunders the early evening

Clouds dim the daytime

Magical contrast for streaks of electricity flashing from sky to ground

Sidewalks empty

Pools closed

Storms

Perfect disrupters to punctuate summer's perfection

Idols and Iconoclasts

Break down the symbols and statues

Erect and venerate new symbols and statues

Choose what to sanctify and what to dismantle

One day, endure the bitter personal destruction of your own legacy

Prop yourself up as an idol and icon

Unworthy at the end to receive even one second of remembrance

Achieve neither fame nor infamy

Lost to the history of cultural descendants who cast their ancestors into the spiritual fire

You did the same

Why did you expect different treatment after constructing a civilizational Frankenstein?

You spit on the past

The future erases any semblance of your worth

Deeming you unworthy of spit

Mimes and Mummies

Social media gyrators

Mimes without the charm, wit, or face paint

Bathing in narcissism

Dancing without elegance or purpose

Lifelike, but wrapped in ego to mimic mummified pharaohs

Gods and Goddesses

Why not the ruler of your own universe?

You are everything

You are the center

Anything that makes you happy

No matter the trail of animosity and damage you leave in your wake

Receive the accolades and worship

Through your mercy you can bestow pardons and favors

Ah, but in truth you have become nothing other than a personified demon

Joining the ranks of the gods and goddesses you fight for control over followers

Immortality reveals itself as an illusion

Goodnight forever

You demon

Doppler Affect

Relationships move into focus rapidly as they approach you

As you approach them

The same relationships move out of focus just as quickly as they trail away

And as you trail away

Fleeting moments with those meant to help you sharpen your recognition of hereditary sights and sounds

Fleeting moments to fine tune your spiritual antennae

Hot Nothingness

Summer heat rains down on the uninspired as they seek to quell their restlessness

Pour the next margarita and crack open the next beer

Tunes of tired new songs erase the consciousness

No love

No caring

No meaning

Just a mad search for relevancy among the irrelevant

Autumn waits to follow summer and bestow its own seasonal festivities upon the unconscious

Halloween, Oktoberfest, leaves leaching color

Similar Opposites

One man with no drive to do anything

Watches the same shows repeatedly

Finds jobs and revels in complaining about them

Never takes any risks

Claims how hard he works

How hard he's always worked

Judges in conversation

Mocks silently in or outside the company of others

Lives in a state of misery that distorts his face with every passing year

A second man claims the drive to strike out on his own

He races around to, during, and from work

Talks of the day he will become successful

Taking action with increasing hesitancy as time progresses

Never takes any risks

Enjoys the consistency of doing what he does not like

Judges on the phone

Mocks in person

Lives in a state of fearful momentum that disguises itself as conscientiousness

The first man crawls in circles as the second man flies in them

The circles overlap

Neither man moves outside his radius

Two men

Similar opposites

Worse than Cain's Sacrifice?

We sacrifice truth and sincerity at the altar of the postmodern gods

Nothing heartwarming do we receive in return

We seek immortal internal peace from those that cannot grant it to us

Clamoring to become gods ourselves

Yielding what's best in us and stamping out the light in our brothers in the process

Envy pervades the postmodern gods and their followers like

The growing band of followers eventually sacrifice society at the altar

Society gives up the ghost

Grudges

Grudges do far worse than keep a man fixated on that which prevents him from advancing

Fixations carry him backward to angers, regrets, and additional grudges that snowball upon the current grudges

Though seemingly in the present

He transports himself back in time and traps himself in the avalanche of loathing

Seeking to reorient the past to prevent the perceived or actual slight

This adventure with time travel cannot deliver on any figments of truth congealed in the grudge-holders mind

Self-righteousness escapes through holes in the snowscape of loathing

Pomposity finds a home in the present and a nursing home in the future

Arrogant Son of a Bitch

Cast your net of sorrow around those who long ago moved on from your mutual history

Mutual history for which you play movie reels in the recesses of your mind

Projected onto screens of your burned out modern day

You imagine the accomplished as being your spiritual enemies

Enemies worthy of your friendship if you can inflict hesitation in their actions to do what you could never dream

Your vigor died in the town you still exalt as the environment that defines you

The town will define you even as your purported enemies untangle the net of sorrow you cast

Your attempts to shackle your adversaries have shackled you with rage at their growth

Rage will imprison you as you shadowbox with your own entrenched demons of arrogance

The Guilted Age

You will accept the punishment

Whether or not you deserve it

Learn nothing

Earn nothing

Follow your masters

Anticipate their dictates

No absolution for your dissolution

No exploration permitted beyond the barriers of dishonesty

Swallow the guilt you are force fed

Ingest the guilt into your stream of unconsciousness

Welcome to the Guilted Age

Ostracize

Individual thought

In short supply

Forces the practitioner onto the journey of becoming a ghost

Shapeless and ostracized.

Resumes human form to haunt those bent on castigating him from their high yet crumbling moral towers

Discombobulated

Currents of inadequacy nearly sweep her away to open waters of pain and disappointment

A riptide of hopelessness almost drowns her

Swimming perpendicular to the riptide

Then toward the distant shore

Seeking a vessel to survive the sharks lurking below and all around

Just Visiting

Visit my old town at the ocean

No longer home

Experience the sights and sounds of visitors and residents alike

Almost a wrap on July

Little over a month for the tourist and homesteader to bury their cares in the sand

Shops and eateries demand you lose yourself in the beauty of your surroundings

Forget the costs and diminished values

Forget the hospitality staff salivating over your money

Engaging you in drivel more meaningless than their superficial smiles

Traveled to the town

Lived there

Moved

Traveled there again

Short-lived home

Long-lived appreciation for leaving it

Off the Cusp

Cross the threshold of something great

Or teeter at the brink and fall backwards

Nearing the point where nobody can pull you away from destiny

Never reaching that point

Asking permission from those with no stake in your quest

Never to cross the threshold until you stop asking permission

Achilles Rupture

Weak spots in spiritual and physical armors gave way

An Achilles rupture coincided with the reversal of maturation

Dipped in the river of grace years earlier

Refusing to fully submerge

Still sore every now and again

Achilles tendon healed with surgery and time

The spiritual Achilles needed more time to immerse in the enchanted waters

Generational Peace

What good can pass down through the generations?

One form of inheritance

Peace of mind secured by surrendering grievances

What rotting of an individual occurs when harboring resentments for a time in which he did not live?

Trapped in a past he uses to justify his anger for all time

Sinister transmission of hatreds that freeze descendants in permanent rage

How difficult to maintain serenity, even without continued resentment toward the past

Praying for rage to be more ephemeral than peace of mind

Putting the Flying Carpet before the Pegasus

A difficult task

The Pegasus must pull the flying carpet

Or else

Winged-horse crashes to the ground when the carpet leads the flight

Summer Waves

Ocean waves roll forward this mid-August day

The ripples swim to the shoreline, splashing all the happy beachgoers in their path

Boogie borders and sunbathers, absorbing the future recollections that only summer can bring

Cool breezes lurk around summer's corner

August joy of parents' tranquility and children's laughter lasts forever

Myrtle Beach

Immersed in the warm and magnetic ocean along the South Carolina coast

No interest in boardwalks, shopping, rides, events, pools, restaurants, or bars

No search for a vacation fix to numb me to everyday life

Just playing in the water

To link to the life energy that feeds my time and purpose

Dangerous Resurrection

When you resurrect friends from the graves of dead friendships, you use an unnatural power

You take on a savior complex as nauseating as a man trying to change a woman into something she's not

As nauseating as a woman who tries to change a man into something he's not

You have no power to change the soul

No power to revive friendships

None of the powers you pretend to possess

Angels dare not go where you tread in desperation

You have no wings

No gavel

None of what you need to regain what you lost

Merely a longing for impossibilities

Careful what you dig up

You won't revive dead friendships, but you will resuscitate gremlins from the abyss

Mirage

Figment of a self-destructive imagination

Moving closer, there's nothing to replenish the weary traveler

Just an excruciating heat to trick the driver into looking for an unreachable oasis

Keep driving from one mirage to the next

Live Your Truth

The mantra of the day, "live your truth!"

Inspires millions

Devotees of themselves

Self-respect?

Striving?

Unique purpose?

What a crock

Adulation replete with hollow rituals in the corners of worried minds

Rituals for those who devote themselves to themselves

Live your truth!

No individualism

An insincere dedication

Unanchored by any decent, timeless force

A personal vision of love

Fleeting, yet as explosive as an afternoon summer storm in the Rockies

A collective of vacuous vessels

Claiming individuality despite a mindset damned to the most typical and bankrupt actions

Ahhhh, how liberating to separate from spiritual laws

The caricature becomes a distinct lord of a distinct universe

All a sham

Follows others and remains bound by collectivist dogmas

All at once, a separate universe

Lord of that universe

Follower of a doomed collective

Priests of the religion encourage their followers' illusions

Sinister advice

Cloaked beneath a veneer of guidance

Live your truth!

Recipe for destruction

Devotees thrust collateral damage on those they claim to love

The mantra must hold at any price

Live your truth

Absorb your horrors

Self-worship and self-actualization of the self-oppressed collective

Beleaguered Elephant

The beleaguered elephant trudges across the grasslands

His herd leaves

Lions and hyenas surround him

Wild creatures close in

Even civilized creatures hunt the elephant

Scavengers wait to feed on him

None seek his tusks or his trunk

They simply want him dead and decomposed

The beleaguered elephant

Neither king of the jungle nor pig in the mud

Just a creature with no house or tribe

Embarking on a hazardous solitary journey across the savannah

You Eat Bugs, I'll Eat Spaghetti

You tell me I'm selfish for wanting to eat delicious food

Would you not permit me a nice plate of fresh spaghetti?

You want me to eat bugs as part of your efforts to rule me

Do you realize I know you don't care about conservation or clean resources?

You pressure me to worship the climate that you pretend I can destroy

You, I gather, will be exempt from your own dictates

They are dictates, are they not?

What you want turns into what you require

All for your power games

I will not submit

Go eat bugs

I'll eat spaghetti

You're for the Little Guy?

You believe in helping the little guy

So you say

You want to help the little guy

The downtrodden

The underdog

Help them at everyone's expense

Including the other little guys

The downtrodden

The underdogs

Prepackaged antipathy, resentment, and dependence

Your tax-free donations to the little guy

You lecture from the safety of your community as you help destroy theirs

How does it feel to become a big shot who pisses all over the downtrodden you claim to support?

Moral encouragement for the movements and measures impoverishing society at all levels

Not for David

You're for Goliath and all his ilk

You arrogant charlatan

The Chasm

The chasm grows

Unbridgeable

Conversations now worth nothing

Different mindsets entirely

An illusion of togetherness rockets across the night sky

Into the depths of space

Opposing sides dug into the fields of righteousness

No common ground

Growing chasm

The only common space between the antithetical sides

Reflections of the Wicked

The wicked stare into the void

No mirrors in front of them or pools of water for them to watch
or wash their faces

Just a cosmic mirror reflecting the images of wilted beings

No facelifts or adornments can mask the decrepit nature of self-adulation

A collection of gods and goddesses stares into the void

Feel their own wrath

Hear their voices bouncing back to them within the great cosmic echo chamber

The gods and goddesses, idols of their own making

They bask in their rule as they drain life energies from mere mortals

A vainglorious panoply of wannabe supernaturals

The wicked wonder why they continue to shrivel before the Light

Reflections of matter that decompose in the heavens

The Ship already Crashed

The ship smashed into the giant mountain protruding from the sea floor

Many passengers injured

Crew acted as though no impact occurred

Passengers awaited the promise of a smooth ride

Interrupted by a purposeful course correction into the monstrous and visible structure

A mountain, crashed ship, and swelling sea

Passengers in denial

A drunken captain, high on the bizarre allure of a seafaring disaster

Fixated on destroying the ship, the captain and crew, royal as they were, fled the ship on their life rafts

Passengers, deluded and frightened, left to die or swim for survival on the high seas of tragedy

Tropical Marvel to Tropical Decimation

The most beautiful island

A scenic marvel in the spring

A warm and serene energy encapsulates the Floridian paradise

Tropical fauna and flora populate the land and sky amid the gently splashing waters

Autumn arrives

The Gulf of Mexico, overtaken by a counterclockwise whirling phenomenon

A cyclone of obliteration fractures the natural and manmade topography

The inhabitants prepare to rebuild as the cyclone could not pierce the human spirit

Despite the decimation, the flooded island promises to once again bring forth great beauty

People, animals, and vegetation ready themselves to make it so

Music of Seaside Heights, Then and Now

The boardwalk welcomes the last crowds of the season

Games and rides disappear in plain sight

Cool air resurfaces as memories rekindle an old summer that never was

The woman I should have married passed nearly a decade ago

Her spirit lives on

I stroll the boardwalk

Speakers from the side streets, cars, bars, and nightclubs play music reminiscent of my times with her

As if she has a remote control to orchestrate the soundtrack of the evening

In the past, I was never big on frequenting the shoreline

It's a place I should've walked with my girlfriend and held her hand in the summer sun

For this boardwalk stroll, her spirit takes my hand and reminds me of who I am, who I was, and who I should be

The music continues

Apple Picking Alone

For the first time in your travels, you wonder what people think of you

They might ask themselves, "who is this man who travels alone at a place not known for the solitary traveler?"

They probably ask themselves nothing at all about you, because your existence too is hardly noticeable

You picked some excellent apples

It's just that picking them alone is hardly worth the taste of your companionless harvest

Autumn Reigns Supreme

Autumn steals the crown

Raw winds ossify the bones of summer's faithful adherents

The adherents turn into begrudging serfs with allegiance to their new fall master

All hail autumn, wild and howling king for the next three moons

Tantalizing Seductress of Belonging

Tantalizing seductress of belonging, you tempt us with your warm embrace

An embrace that turns cold and freezes our senses

You order us to obey, under punishment of permanent isolation

We declare our independence, united in common cause against you

Mighty seductress, we take satisfaction

Knowing that you, without earning sorrow or tribute, will decompose in your coffin of failure

An Ode to the Physical World

Something real in an era of virtual life

The physical world manifests in food

In shelter

Clothing

In fellow human beings

Linked to spirit and materialism, the physical world exists.

In a time of virtual thoughts

Virtual feelings

Virtual relationships

Tangible life provides hope and meaning to gracious inhabitants

Let the physical world be a God-given rock to overcome virtual disconnectedness

EXILED (POEMS III)

A lamo

The valiant make their last stand to defend the grounds they treasure

Not everybody can summon the rustic courage to defend land, people, or principles

Some men never have a defining moment at their own outpost of existence

One way or another, all men find themselves in Alamo territory

Their actions, in light of no reinforcements, determine rallying cries for the ages

Or silence in cages

Back to Tennessee

Back to Tennessee after 14 months

This time an October trek

The Great Smoky Mountains

Vibrant tree colors through the valley

Raining leaves on mystical paths across the misty wilderness

A resilient energy of independence

A torrential downpour arrives as the remnants of summer heat fade into a bitter cold

Travelers revel in the scenery's grandeur and hospitality

Tennessee, the soul of a vast region east of the Mississippi

The pioneering spirit radiates throughout the skies and tributaries

A spirit homesteading in the hills and forests

Diminishing Resources

Stare into your minuscule screens and live a life without connection

Stay at home and accept your lot in life

Follow the overproduced and under-spirited music we command you to enjoy

Do you not know that real entertainment is for those who can afford it?

What can you afford?

No fancy dining for you

No celebrations beyond the meager ones your worthless earnings can provide

Enjoy the memories of past travels, dinners, movies, shows, and concerts

Your future memories will be what we allow them to be

Watch us as we steal your resources and deliver them to those we deem worthy

Thank you for your obedience

Oh, how we do appreciate you, the most compliant of our dispirited followers

A Short Break from Italian

A brief period away from the Italian food of the mid Atlantic

Nothing better than Southern Italian dishes sprinkled with North Jersey style

But difficult to turn away from the Tennessee barbecue

Bring on the savory steaks, skewered shrimp, and mouth-watering river trout

Back to calamari marinara soon enough

In the meantime, dining by moonshine

A hot biscuit in my hands

Faint sounds of bluegrass on my mind

This culinary excursion too shall pass

Memories of the Tennessee experience will resurface someday

Someday, while chowing down on lasagna

Someday, back in the hustle and traffic horns of the mid Atlantic

Extended Warmth

Walking the suburban Tennessee neighborhood on a warm October day

Sunlit streets line the growing development

Children playing carefree in the driveways and on the sidewalks

Halloween decor greets the stroller with lawn displays reminiscent of previous decades

Only 8 days until Halloween

No chill today in this region of the Volunteer State

Northeastern temperatures can fluctuate for a while as the heart
of fall approaches

Temperatures fluctuate in Tennessee as well

But the enchanting skies east of Nashville supply extended heat

Connecting the recently deceased summer to the embryonic
winter

Everyone's a Stranger

Nobody familiar

No comforting eyes, comforting smiles, or comforting words

Out of place

Sensing the animosity

Absorbing the anger

Hearing the hissing

House of bipolarity

Patrons of icy disposition

Ravenous sharks

Stokers of unquenchable flames

Heat turned up, but still as cold as can be

Humans with no warmth

Part men and part buzzards

People trapped in the blizzard of a comatose existence

The saloon of wasted life

Customers drunk on fermented memories

Swashbuckling mind trips

Traipsing inebriated along the minefields

A tipsy collection of slovenly bravados

Stashing bottles of lost time

Hungover on hang-ups

Dependence on intoxicating pain

You

Me

Them

Everyone's a stranger

Another Restaurant Flailing in the Wind

The great German restaurant

Filled with lively music and entertainment

Bustling with patrons

Friendly staff

Excellent ambience

Top-notch Spätzle

Golden potato pancakes

Succulent potato salad

Mouthwatering goulash

One year later and a new atmosphere pervades the establishment

Sparse crowds

No music or entertainment

Staff waiting for the shift to end

Sour faces

Subpar spätzle

Discolored potato pancakes

Uninspired potato salad

Underwhelming goulash

From the great German restaurant to the diminished German restaurant

Requiem for another restaurant flailing in the wind

I Seek Justice!

I seek justice to ignore my own shortcomings

As a substitute for religion

Less purpose in my life than I care to admit

I seek justice to become a creator of heaven and earth

To dispense my wrath at those that do not follow the pathway I prescribe for enlightenment

Because of my addiction to emotional tyranny

I manipulate myself and all others

Twisting reality to maintain intellectual superiority

I seek justice to lose my humanity

Enforcing a bastardized version of humanity onto society

To revolutionize civilization

To levy blame

Avoid atonement

Having no happiness in my soul

A vacuous being

Lusting for accolades

I seek justice

Or so I claim

Wanting nobody to ever really have it

Music

Music everywhere!

Not a symphony or ensemble

No ballads or instrumentals

No classical or country

Silent music in unseen kaleidoscopic patterns

Arrangements promise danger or joy

A soundtrack to life

Metronomes and harmonies reveal themselves in heartbeats

At work and at play

In dreams and aspirations

Visions and purpose

Suddenly, an amalgamation of cacophonies coalesces

Time to observe the conductor

As he recalibrates the blend of tones and rhythms for symbiosis with all his surroundings

Listening to the band and the orchestra

Using all six senses

Letting the volume diminish when discordant noises threaten the ongoing invisible concert

Silent music

Seeking silent music in everything

Witnessing the power of a flawless conductor who pieces together a harmonic story

To follow anytime and anywhere

Stone-Blooded Sucker

Medusa stares through my skin and cartilage to freeze my heart

My body solidifies when observing her alluring ugliness

She whispers to me the secrets of her deceit

Her snakes swim about her head and hiss at me as I turn into an ill-fated statue of obedience

Obedience to a power that molds me through beauty, hideousness, and guile

Bereft of autonomy, my life turns to stone for all to see

Buried alive in an unceremonious mausoleum

A mausoleum fabricated by the eyes of Medusa

The mortal Gorgon sister encases me for all time in an upright coffin

No Pegasus will spring forth from the creature that manufactured my untimely grave

Singer's Conversation with the Audience

She sings to talk with the audience

It's the best way she knows to communicate with a crowd

And she's good at it

She radiates feelings of pain, invisible to the casual observer

Lackluster family support

Dashed dreams of a husband that almost was and children that never were

Her motivation to unleash her talents carries on

She seeks the elusive warmth of people that have none

The show closes

Cheering dies off for the evening

A painful silence reminds her of the family bonds she does not have

She experiences the agonizing reminder every night as she exits stage left

With nobody waiting to greet her

Pianos for All

You watch people and can hear their music

Their piano most of all

Ragtime

Classical

Jazz

Rock

Soft melodies

Loud bursts of anti-music

Piercing horror

Intricate songs, with or without depth

Sad chords

Mysterious scales

Almost always fusions of different tunes

Sometimes flat and sometimes sharp

Other times right on key

Now and again

The pitch reveals a synchronicity with the rhythms of celestial
orbits and rotations

Revealing an improvisational alignment with cosmic bodies

And at unforeseen moments

Illiquid tonalities reveal the warping of time and space as you
approach the event horizon

Most pianos need a tune-up

Or you're not receiving the melodies correctly

Your receptors need a tune-up

Vision merges with sound

Pianos drive the compositions

And the universe makes a little more sense than it would without the black and white keys

Instrumentals

Listen to a person's drums, guitars, cellos, and saxes

You can glimpse different sides of a person you miss as you focus on the person's piano

With a great appreciation for music

You hear a person's entire band or symphony

You hear the person's sections of an orchestra

You envisage the concert

First violin

Second violin

A group of separate instruments not made for concertos

You might not see the person's conductor

Though you get to hear the fruits of the conductor's work

To observe and listen

You will never be the same after hearing people's instruments and musical arrangements

Piano Bar or More?

The piano bar player makes his mark

Sings with hearty joy

Brings smiles and cheer to the nightly crowds

His talents appreciated by the audiences who see him

His talents unknown to the audiences who never know he exists

Back at Sea

On a ship in the middle of the ocean

Physical simulation for sailing across the heavens

Light waves splash the vessel as time and gravity splash into a
space shuttle

Wave frequencies change at sea and beyond the atmosphere

Stars provide a natural compass, while floating across the water
and floating across outer space

An electrifying allure at sea of what creatures my ship could pass

Cloud formations and sunsets distinguish the waters I traverse

The cosmos, I imagine composed of flowing expanses of dark liquid water

Water within which animals can swim from one celestial body to another

My time at sea

An adventure on planet Earth

A taste of travel through the heavens

Whales

From the ship's balcony, I stare at the ripples across the water

My mind records videos of the sea for recollections long after my return to dry land

Sunlight shines beneath the cumulus-painted skies

Scattering a mist of aqua to spotlight the ocean's main attraction

The blue whale launches above the surface

Leading his devoted pod along a vast and adventurous pelagic zone

Golden Apple

The golden apple brings happiness to every sight and bite

Radiant flavor and delicious color

Such a simple fruit to find and eat

Scattered about trees and fields

Ready for the picking and lasting for many seasons

No seasoning required to draw out the taste

No mixtures or dressings needed

Not a guilt-infused calorie in the golden apple's natural state

No serpent slithering or whispering for you to take what you should not have

No remorse for exploring open orchards

A rare occurrence for remorse to find a home in a raw golden apple

Fair warning would be granted

One bite of the encouraged fruit does much to replenish

A bite that restores the hungry

A bite that refreshes the spirit and feeds the mind

With a leftover core and leftover pits that replenish the land

As long as golden apples populate the Earth, man has a fighting chance at life

Space and Time, a Heavenly Brotherhood

Space has a lifelong friendship with time

Where you find one, you find the other

When you find one, you find the other

A friendship born during creation

Outlasting the imaginations of the most ambitious stars and planets

True compadres that guide the galaxies

Directing objects smaller than electrons and events larger than supernovas

Space and time revere one another

A shared understanding found in countless frequencies across the heavens

As long as one lives, they both live

As one dies, they both die

Two friends that could not bear the death of the other

Space and time are twins

Their bonds of affection and lasting lives show the meaning of quantum brothers, not star-crossed lovers

Cold

Winter spreads frost and melancholy across the land

The dead of winter

Trees stripped of leaves

People stripped of ambition

Frigidity found in the frozen zest for life

Kinetic energy loses fluidity in the thoughts of men and the instincts of beasts

Snow falls as ice blocks of time prolong the winter

The season refuses to allow solid ground to thaw or embittered feelings to soften

The Christmas spirit gets stowed away, shelved until year's end

Until year's end, when winter returns with cyclical, fleeting novelty

The here and now in the dead of winter brings little glee

A juncture of hardships and regrets

Daily doses of sunlight offer delusions of comfort

Whistling clouds and growling winds deny heat to the hopeful

Winter cold slices through the towns and cities

Winter cold embedded in the icy hearts of frozen men

Rough Waters

Turbulence on the emerald open seas for me and my ship

Lightning pours with occasional flashes of rain across my cabin
window

A green lightning dampened yet framed by the mist

Steady winds restore the waves into rhythm with the sky

Until the winds disrupt the patterns of the sea

The stretch of ocean brings disharmony between air and water

My ship suffers the consequences of titanic forces

The vessel adjusts to the waters, and so must I

I must bear the burden of leaving my port

Life away from land and all of land's common obstacles

Off to a world of a shifting medium

Nowhere to step off my ship except to sink into the raging ocean
waves

Far from any ports and islands, I seek the significance of my odyssey

No Homeric myth can I envision

Finding myself capsized by swells of doubt about whether I can ever pilot back

Adventure on the ocean to discover my home

The sea beneath lifts my vessel from the water and throws me from my chair

Roaring currents threaten to deliver me to my final resting place in the afterworld

Remember

Never forget!

Quickly forgotten

Warnings fail

Generations lost

Many Coffins

Virus looms

Paranoia spreads

Society loses

Join the cultural graveyard

The Climate Monster Is Everywhere... Almost

A drop of rain falls in the desert

It must be climate change

A cheetah kills a gazelle and laughs at his conquest

It must be climate change

A matador slips on a banana peel for the fifth time in a day

It must be climate change

A whore house closes, angering the local bingo club

It must be climate change

Hailey's Comet flies through a wormhole

It must be climate change

Ghosts from King Arthur's Court open up a food truck

It must be climate change

Drive-in movie theaters offer half-off discounts to barber shop quartets

It must be climate change

A community of people is happy and helpful, driven and creative

It must be... absolutely must be... white supremacy

Eyes of the Followers

Eyes emptier than the largest vacuum of space

Old friends and adversaries alike

Once filled with the energies of uplifting traditions and sober actions

Now they guard the words they utter with greater zeal than the Cyclops longs for the flesh of man

Eyes bewildered by self-inflicted obsessions

Old friends and adversaries follow speech codes with frenzied orthodoxy

Uplifting traditions and sober actions die from willful suicides of the spirit

The modern Cyclopes, each with an evil eye

An evil eye maladjusted to light in their wretched caves of sanctimonious deviance

The Last Cherries

My last cherries for the season

The final bowl carries a hint of sadness amidst the delight

As August moves forward, the quality of the cherries deteriorates

Heartwarming to have a delectable batch and savor the flavor through fall, winter, and spring

Next June will bring fresh bowls

Bags of Bing and Rainier will refresh my palate once again

Until next summer, I wish my favorite fruit a magical hibernation

Where To?

Worries amounted to nothing worthwhile

Schooling led to nothing sustainable

Athletics yielded nothing impressive

Music brought forth nothing notable

Performing in an empty theater

Wondering where the spirit train will travel

Seeking the end of isolation

Looking for pastures greener than hopes from yesteryear

Which Way to the Garden?

Dismember civilization

Dismantle culture

Desecrate traditions

Defile institutions

Damage families

Degrade individuals

Discombobulate souls

Damn us all to fall like dominoes

Broken

Cultural strain cracked the already tenuous ties of affection
among relatives

No meeting of the minds or the spirits

All that remained was contempt

Common historical ties broke permanently, creating new tribes across the familial tundra

Flummoxed

Ideas shrivel

Voices mute

Actions cease

Once great megalopolis

Sinks into the quicksand of societal fear

Once great souls

Burn in the fiery morass

The slaughtered endure perpetual trials in absentia from life

Venom

Venom dripping from their snarling mouths

An obsession so grim it frightens the mirror into which they
gaze

Living lives steeped in envy

Embracing jealousies they cultivate with like-minded malcon-
tents

Lost Civilization

Here's to inhabitants of a lost civilization

They built magical structures

Wrote inspiring music

Told tales that transcended their mortality

Engineered unsurpassed medical wonders

Short-lived successes in the record books of geologic time scales

Microscopic accomplishments in the astronomic chronologies

Three cheers to the individuals of a lost civilization

Legends worthy of admiration through the millennia

Spirits dishonored and disemboweled by demonic mutilators

The Filmmaker

They wish to edit the story of your life into a clichéd tragedy of their own making

Preferring to observe your failures than to perform as actors on their own stages

They cannot produce

They cannot edit

They cannot write

Critiquing, and nothing more

Their stages crumble with every passing hour

Unleashing your own story, you will abolish their directorial dictates

Independence

July 4th will always be special

A remarkable and unbreakable connection to Passover

A yearning for independence matched with an obligation for independence

Another bond between the ancient Israelites and the American founding

The story of Moses, inexorably linked with Washington, Adams, Jefferson

Passover, more God's story than Moses's

Independence Day, more God's story than Washington's, Adam's, or Jefferson's

Freedom granted by God

Codified in word and action

By the descendants of Jacob

And the descendants of a modern Western tradition

Parting the Red Sea

Crossing the Delaware

Different stories in different places and different times

And yet the same stories in different places and different times

The spirit of Zion took a transatlantic journey to the original thirteen colonies

The spirit remains

Dining Out

Dining out among the commoners became a casualty of a culture losing its way

Opulent fools continued to eat in their desired growing isolation from the societal decay

Societal decay swallowed the deluded fools.

Gluttons of arrogance digested by the lord of the ghouls

Pole Vault

A pole vaulter prepares for his jump

Society sets the bar higher and higher in the middle of his leap

The ground underneath hardens from soft matting to hard stone

The man cannot clear societal hurdles while the physics of civilization break down

He died upon landing, joining former athletes turned into current corpses

Momentous

From a hopeless realm

The portal of faith appears

Tyranny vanquished

A civilization reborn

Camaraderie

Family and friendships disappear.

The days of feasts and events move into recollections

Recollections resurrected by minds trapped in emptiness

Camaraderie slips away

Dreams of close bonds evaporate in all seasons and temperatures

No more get-togethers at the old houses from a time now dead and buried

Faded

What happened to the old family events?

They faded, as did the love and warmth surrounding them

Nostalgia cannot rekindle those past connections

Cousins freeze you out

Aunts and uncles pretend you never existed

The memories turn to shadows of a time that history ingested

Extended family spurns you for your adherence to hallowed traditions

Such is the price for standing against their hollowed conventions

Parameters

Old friends, weakened bonds

Offensive conversations off limits

The new normal of our discussion parameters

Shatter these parameters

NINE LIVES (POEMS IV)

Carnival

The sights and sounds of summer

Meandering through time

Clear visions of strolls along the boardwalks

Fireworks and festivities ingrained in the fabric of life

June passes

July dissipates

August melts

But the ice creams, zeppoles, rides, and light-ocean surf last forever

Civilizational Star Path

The civilizational star moves through the course of its life

Lighter elements fuse and the core shines with increasing yet life-sustaining intensity

The star's gravity pulls in the best of the celestial thinkers

Gravity dwindles, and the core runs out of fuel

The star cannot recharge, and it dies an explosive death.

The remaining cultural black hole sucks in all the societal energy

Stars live, and stars die

So do civilizations

Super Rebel

Lonely narcissism reigns supreme in the super rebel

Synonymous with the sycophantic groupie

Never living in the spirit of independence

The Endangered Diner

The diner became an endangered species

Menus with endless arrays of pages

Fries with enough ketchup to fill your heart's content

Burgers with crunchy pickles and sides of coleslaw that tasted better at midnight than noon

Triple decker sandwiches or the anytime syrup-laden breakfasts

Change for the jukebox

Vibrant meetups

Profound discussions

Post-event stopovers before the anti-climactic arrivals home

All of it threatened by emergency mandates

Fewer places

Reduced hours

Traditions under assault

The diner, on the verge of extinction, along with everything else

Grimy

Bipeds swimming in barnyard mud

Jumping in from a diving board

Wading through the sludge

Filth cakes into the pores

Grimy with pride

Slimy on all sides

Burials

Welcome to the killing fields

Once treasured legacies, strewn all over the ground Some

memories buried

Others left unburied for the vultures of misery to devour

Discarded

You speak your mind too many times

All aboard the boxcar

Crammed in

Horrific labors await

The locomotive trails off into the distance

Your life trails off into hell

Empty Shelves

Missing brands

Inflated prices

Reduced package volumes

Confounded shoppers

Stressed communities

Society moving backwards

Empty shelves

The product of empty suits and empty souls

.

Ignorant Pride

Charlatans with self-righteous intellect

Superiority complexes with which they adorn themselves

Phony humility becomes them

Consumed by thoughts of standing valiantly on the edge of history

Ideas stretch beyond their capacity for realization

Seers without sight

Seekers without depth

Listeners without discernment

Men with ignorant pride

Peering from lofty towers built on everlasting wreckage

Arrogant Naïveté

The power of arrogant naïveté

Directing disbelief toward talk of uncomfortable truths

Mistaking concern for complaining

Understanding for negativity

Awareness for hatred

Passion for rage

And honesty for hyperbole

Arbiters of positivity and polite conversation

Self-proclaimed neutral parties, interested in resolutions

As long as the resolutions spare them any reflection of the consequences

Unwitting dupes of wicked forces

Arrogant naïveté, a necessary condition for death camps

College?

Stay away from the university system!

Colleges brainwash

Professors stupefy

Administrators cower

Students inflict vengeance

Look at all the worthless degrees

Check out the wackos walking around campus

Notice the crazy theater productions

Witness the decline in readings of the great books

Also...

You must go to college

To figure out what you want

To socialize you

For opening doors

College, the saving grace for a person's life

The fallback for learning

Go to college and tempt hell, because what else could you possibly accomplish as a sovereign individual?

When you graduate, join us in lambasting the system we love to hate

The Duck Pond and Its Companions

Travel back to the old duck pond

Nestled in a quiet suburb

Surrounded by grass, flowers, weeping willows, and oaks

Small shops, wooded neighborhood blocks, and beautiful houses

An extinct train station and defunct railroad tracks

A little bridge over the duck pond accentuated the view from the benches

Back as a young child, my family brought me there to read and watch the ducks

The weeping willows bore witness over these eternal moments in a child's life

The old duck pond, a slice of nature carved out from the urban behemoth

A friend's house nearby, whose backyard contained a pond of its own

A backyard pond for swimming humans and fish alike

Refreshing on a hot summer day... much like the blast of his house's air conditioning

All the heat that drenched you dissipated at first encounter with the magical AC

Deer traversed the backyard grass, visible from the deck and zip line's panorama

Space and time intertwine in ways that seem indistinguishable

Memories that meld the geography and history of your life

The old duck pond, a portal to an era and location steeped in happiness

The River of Psychosis

The River of Psychosis has not crested

Troubles have just begun

Passengers on a ship across this turbulent river of nightmares

Tributaries wider, longer, and deeper than the voluminous ocean of your worst fears

Let Him steer the ship to grant you safe passage through the flood

After making it to the other side, look for the dove

And see the eagle soar once again

The Delusion of an Open Mind

An open mind, with no semi-permeable membrane to filter out destructive tendencies

Just a Maginot Line against annihilation

No way to ingest and absorb decent ideas

The thin layering dissipates, and so does the individual

All Hail Envy!

To the lions at your beck and call!

Thumbs up for those whose possessions and livelihoods you allow

Thumbs down for those you loathe

Envy, ending in the death of souls and civilizations, including your own

October 31st

The joys of autumn

Pumpkin carving

Cider tasting

Crisp air

Celebration not of death, but of life

Life before the yearly hibernating force of winter

Life before haunted hay rides turn into snow-packed sleigh rides

Train Loop and Beyond

The train circles much of the park

A park for the ages

Petting zoo

Watching zoo

Playground

Picnic area

Fields

Seeing ostriches and lambs

Riding the train adds a special dimension to walking the same areas

All aboard!

Embark on the loop path around a treasured park

Not all perfect moments or memories, from the playground to the cafeteria

But all the memories carry entrenched lessons

Experiences from the trains of old

Hop on some trains in the current day

Maybe even become a conductor

Seeking new grounds to explore and visions to unleash

The Lake

Home away from home

Yearly fireworks as the boaters permeate the lake and cheer on the grand finale

Clean, cool water to bathe in under the sizzling skies

Village resting in the shade of tree canopies populating a rural outpost of the suburbs

Flora, green and multicolored, stretch across the land to the shore banks

Docks and rowboats abound

House on a magical island

Backyard lake, flanked by foothills

The warmth of a northeastern clan

A rare species of people with the sincerity and love of a bygone era

Feasts

Barbecues

Wholesome laughs

A lake ensconced in promise

A time soon betrayed by cultural fault lines

In Vain?

Has it all been for nothing?

The dead and wounded from the Revolutionary War

Hundreds of thousands of Civil War casualties

Revolts against segregation with mind, body, and spirit

Defeating socialist empires

Corruption of arts, sciences, and advancements in human history

Cynically infused cultural self-doubt becomes palpable

The taste of the self-doubt, nauseating

A powerful culture spoils on the vine

The firmly rooted tree of civilization decomposes

What becomes of those who toil and sacrifice for a brighter future?

Sacrifices of great men will never be in vain

Actions of societal murderers will be in vain

Over the long course of geologic time

Warning Signs

Impending destruction

You read the signs

But you do not heed them

Institutions rotting from the inside out

And the outside in

Culture unraveling thread by thread

Evil rituals trample and supplant rich traditions

Universities become insane asylums

Entertainment yields naked perversion

Business turns ideological

Science, stifled by medical witchcraft and pharmaceutical sorcery

Families break apart

Friendships fracture

Your neighbors muzzle themselves

Prices skyrocket

Value vaporizes

Values burn and the embers of life drift away in the night

The signposts warn you

Warning signs, which double as side effects of an expiring culture

Casualties, not Victims

The spiritual war for the future of Western civilization rages

The twisted monsters attempt to impose suffering on you for your mindset

You face the hard truth that you can quickly become a casualty of the intense battles

You suffer material loss

Friends turn away from you

The monsters set the stage for their possessed worshippers and the fearful neutrals to banish you

You become a casualty

A casualty, not a victim

Victims do not always recover, at least not in this life

Casualties, even murdered and banished ones, keep their given purpose and never vanish in vain

Serfdom

Wade through the toxic air of cubicle life

Take orders from managerial automatons

Follow the dictates of HR kings and queens

Bow to professional royalty

Become as backbiting as your fellow serfs

Friday evening arrives

Freedom till Sunday night

The obsequious jitters return

Critical Condition

Dying patient

Irreversible arrhythmia

Reservation for one

Under a patch of soil

Brownshirt

The brownshirt reappears throughout history

During times of malignant spiritual crises

Physical defender of the indefensible

Physical offender who follows the lord of flies

Brute-force arbiter of situations hostile to good judgment

The bully, used by bullies craftier than he

Has moments of glory

Plays a starring and indispensable role in obliterating society

Too clumsy and psychotic to remake society

The weak and brainwashed cower before him

The gods and brainwashers make him disappear...

But only after society cries out to the gods to save them from wanton street violence...

To erase all the pain and inspire false hope

The brownshirt has no lasting home in the present or future

Wherever a rotting society exists, the brownshirt has a temporary home

Until swiftly buried by the forces of good or the gods of evil

Never achieves a lasting glory

Temporary glory filled to the brim with the actions and intentions of unrepentant viciousness

Viciousness lacking the devilish strategy of the brownshirt's cunning, fiendish master

The brownshirt

Has no individual identity

Is what the collective says he is... for a time

Is what the gods and brainwashers say he is and what they allow him to do

Nothing except a casing filled with genocidal rage

Genocidal rage, a purpose all too easily shattered when society regains its bearing

A rage just as easily shattered when the long knives of Satan carve the brownshirt out of the deal

The brownshirt, seen again at spotted moments of future history when called upon to destroy

Every time he takes the bait of his masters

Every time receives no honor or fanfare from anyone

The brownshirt slithers back into the cemetery

Watching the avalanche of history pulverize him in life and death

Stages

Pregnant past

Zygotic present

Embryonic future

Mutual Scavengers

Two friends feed off each other

Maximizing their gains at one another's expense

Each taking a chunk of the other's spirit

Losing his sense of self in the other amid a frenzy of ravenous ingestion

Fighting over nothing, with scraps of themselves rotting on broken plates

Waiting for each other's failures

Patiently

Impatiently

Then, with prodding, to plunge one another into misery

Not rooting for calamity

The harshest tragedies would stifle the superiority complexities should either antagonist suffer permanent defeat

Both men defeated, they lose sight of who is who

Two former friends, now witches who cast spells on one another... and on themselves

Linked for the rest of life in savage wizardry, instead of harmonious kinship

Dismantled

Past evils come to light

New evils emerge to avenge the past ones

This group victimized

Later another

Grudges magnify through the years

The decades

The centuries

As old hatreds fade, the wicked stoke them yet again

Through deceptions

Through the promise of justice

Suffering grows while the bodies pile up

Tectonic plates of anger shift long after the deaths of the victimized

Societies punctuated with bouts of horrors

Societies facing death

Generational feuds dismantle the vestiges of sustainable cultural equilibrium

Grocery Stores

Families rack up their grocery bills

Shocked with outrage

An outrage without physical sight or sound

An outrage felt across the nation as a resonating power

A power without fully formed size or shape

Costs run higher

Availability runs lower

Low enough to spur action

Families bring size and shape to the unstoppable power of their justified intolerance

Idyllic

A Tennessee town

Calling out to the weary traveler

Good energy in the air

People with character and charisma

Surveying the Sunday brunch crowd

Love for family and nation reveals itself in the smiles and serenity

Returning to the down-to-earth town and joint for future brunches

Maybe to visit

Maybe to live

And maybe, just maybe, to rediscover the old spirit of the U.S .A.

New Colors

Beautiful fall colors filled the Smoky Mountains

But what about my own backyard?

The most beautiful colors on a fall foliage trip to Tennessee and North Carolina

Vibrant colors in the valleys, and colors I never recognized before

Returning home, I walked around the neighborhood

Looked with fresh eyes at the leaves

Noticed one of the same deep red colors I saw in the Smokies

Missing the autumn grandeur of the mountains, I found fall beauty in my neighborhood

A beauty I never saw before on my travels

Perhaps my eyes can stay open long enough to notice the deep red leaves in the future

Majesty at home might not match the majesty of travels into the southern mountains

It matters not

Beauty is all around

Let us see what other new colors I can find, right around the corner from home

Life Continues

Life is powerful

There is something about it that people want to continue in themselves and others

A sense of belonging you cannot experience being part of any club or corporation

You have an exclusive membership in life, granted to you by God

People have problems

Inflict problems

Get sick

Die

But for all the ills in the world, people strive to live

During the darkest despairs

In the changing of the guard from older generations to the newer ones

Life continues

Banished

Banishment is rougher than isolation

Thrown out of your psychological neighborhood

Locked in a remote tower

No communication with the banishers

Convicted without evidence

A permanent outcast to those who exile you from their lives

They Took It Away

They took away your travel

They took away your voice

They took away your job

And left you no choice

They took away your purpose

They took away your wife

They took away your home

And crushed your whole life

New Yorkers

Like-minded New Yorkers

The ones that understand the greatness lost in the city we still love

Discussing the five boroughs brings us to a past that has a future in our memories and dreams

New Yorkers forever, with or without the disappearing allure of a once brilliant metropolis

Walking Alone

Circling the Christmas festival around the bay

The town lit up from tree to tree on a blustery night

Strolling alone along the walkways

Detached from many former connections.

With continued life from the one who created me

I am not so alone after all

Jazz

Forming ensembles with friends and family

One day I might have an orchestra

But a superb quartet of great people can work wonders

As can a duo

No matter the numbers

Synching with harmonies and vibrations that dovetail with my purpose

Sometimes heavy metal music runs in the background

I'm keeping jazz playing in the foreground

Wanna Bet?

Novice gambler, 1995

Time to hit the tables and get lucky

Throw away $100 at Blackjack

Draw money from my account

Foreclose on a home and family, 1996

Settling into the shelter

A Very Jersey Cruise

The cruise sets sail from New Jersey

Passengers expose how much they breathe their home state

New Year's Eve, right around the corner

Excitement in the air

Excitement original to the mid-Atlantic

Accents

Mannerisms

Shared love of music

Of food

Of sports teams

And intangible interactions

Connecting forever the residents and common history of the Garden State

Here's to the New Year

Here's to New Jersey

And here's to a very Jersey cruise

Jealous Beast

Within his cave, he deforms himself

Not from flagellation, but from continued emotional scarring over dwelling on those he hates

Claiming proudly that he hates people, and so he hates himself and his friends

His friends, the ones he swarms with bragging that no one else would entertain

Hollow bragging from a hollow and sad little man

Justifying the ugliness on his face as a matter of aging

Aging has nothing to do with the continuous state of competition he has with his friends

Friends he treats like enemies, but he cannot let them go

Without them, he has no one to listen to him, and no one to take for granted

His ugliness grows stronger as he moves from an upright being to a slithering lizard

It's not his complaining that twists him into a beast

It's his desire to drag those surrounding him into a pit of misery

To shovel dust on them and deprive them of the same joy and wonder he deprives from himself

Slithering and slithering, a pathetic reptile

A pathetic reptile who gives up his humanity to judge all people, including the ones who treat him well

He stays in his cave, and his friends rejoice in their freedom from a jealous beast

OVERTIME (POEMS V)

A fter Midnight

Sundry socialites

Dimwitted debutantes

Ornery captains of pretense

Bat shit belles of the ball

Evening turns to early morning

Morning descends into permanent night

The party is over

Your country is gone

The Timing

Two ships passing in the night... along different bodies of water on different planets

"Near misses" became "never in the same galaxies"

Mirages more elusive than any heat-drenched highway blazing through the desert

The Aging

Older relatives move to the next phase of life

They share it with you

You see it

And then you don't see it ever again, when the last phase of life turns into the platform of Hades

Divided

Warring spirits in a spiritual cold war

Fizzing with vengeance

Frothing with envy

Foaming with spite

Fermenting with exasperation

The henchman of the underworld tap dance across the burial ground of goodwill

Dinner Is Served

Old pals prepare a meal

Your soul is the main course

Carved up for all to admire and devour

Racked by Fear

There are those with still-beating hearts

Their voices and actions have become muted by civilization's grim reapers

The reapers reach up from hell to drag all in their path down into the fiery morass of unquenchable misery

Always a step ahead

The demonic shadows keep the naïve and oblivious in a state of mental paralysis

Taking the muted on emotional journeys through the flummoxed space-time of utopian dystopias

The aware flail to rediscover the voices they yielded slowly

Clenching to excuses for why they shriveled into unrecognizable reflections of previously vigorous souls

Grim reapers continue their campaigns of psychological horror and perplexity

As they battle those left with any decency

Once great megalopolises drown in the infernal quicksand of societal fear

Eye of the Hurricane

The hurricane's eye offers respite from the damaging winds

Barricaded within the storm's clearing

Time remains to marshal resources and brace my structure from the system's onslaught

When the eye passes, the sustained gusts will threaten to break my fortifications

I must shield myself from the cyclone

Though with varying intensity and erratic, the system's patterns enable me to prepare

Watching the forecast that I initially ignored

Using the clearing in the hurricane's eye to prevent the erosion
of my solid ground and shelter

Style or Substance?

They called him a fraud

They called him a conman

They called his style arrogant, demeaning, and divisive

It was always his substance they didn't like

It was his actions, his tenacity, and his ability to think for him-
self

They would no less sully a

Docile or uncharismatic man with the same

Ideas or actions as the purported conman they

Hate with an obsession so grim it frightens the mirror in which
they gaze

Venom dripping from their snarling mouths

It's the substance they despise, because they have none

Living lives of quiet jealousy

Finding comfort in an envy they cultivate with like-minded
malcontents

Irreversible

Hatred saturates the land

Mutual loathing ripens and bears poisonous fruit for all

The hatred sustains itself on ghosts of the past, present, and future

There is no escape velocity

Animus infects daily interactions, with no sign of respite or truce

Coldness embeds itself in every morsel of air, mud, and clashing energies

What a Thrill

Marking every checkbox

They often repeat to themselves the phrase, "never settle"

They seek fun, or their ever evolving concept of it, to serve their ego and whims

They seek dinners and events, trips and apparel

And so they use each other for a feeling and for status

Void of any love or substance, they move on with superficiality, crowding out true caring and compassion

They grow older

The thrilled looks on their faces melt away

Substituted by contorted expressions that vacillate between emptiness and disgust

The Filmmaker Redux

Produce the story of your life

A galaxy full of envious and lazy demons descends on every town

Old friends wanting to watch you cannot cushion the landings for all their falls onto the hard floor of misery

They wish to edit your movie into a clichéd tragedy of their own making

They would rather observe your failures than perform as actors on their own stages...

Stages that crumble with every passing hour

Producing the movie of your own life serves as a shield

To enable the dulling and breaking of their continued swords of envy

Detaching from their jealousies and possessiveness brings a satisfaction rarely matched

Unleash your own story, and you will annihilate their onslaught

Friendships Leading to Emptiness

Hanging out with friends leaves you hung out to dry

Chilling with friends leaves you ice cold

Happy hours with friends leave you unhappy

Parties with friends leave you without cheer

Basement

Lowered into a lustful pit of snakes

Now serving serpent desires

Slithering down the spiral staircase

Enslaved in the den of slinking lizards

Dazzling

The flashy wash themselves in showers of praise

Carefully manufactured images of themselves

Garish living for gaudy people

Saturating life to the brim with flaccid spirit

Mutual Burials

You mourn for your meaningful past relationships

But your past friends and family already buried you

They dig your memory up from the grave

You do the same with them

As you wonder how you lost the bonds that brought you to-
gether

The former friends and family already carried on the rituals and
memorial service

Most of them did

Others simply left you unburied

Not cremated either

Left for dead without remembrance or compassion

Even the ones that said their goodbyes with sorrow

They still murdered you

You are dead to them

And they are the ones that put you in the ground

Or left the familial remains of your memory to be scattered across the four corners of nowhere

The next time you think to mourn for your friends

Realize that you already murdered each other

It's just that they probably murdered you first

And moved through the mourning process faster than the speed of deception

Welcome to the killing fields

Once treasured legacies strewn all over the graveyard

Some memories buried

Other memories left unburied for the vultures of misery to devour

Dying Generation, Dying Civilization

The oldest generation has the misfortune of watching Western civilization decay

Those 80 and up lived to see tremendous cultural advance-ments

They created many of them

Now they see zombified intellectuals turn society into something betraying past generations' accomplishments

Contortions of art and science

Soul-numbing music and ideologies

Hackneyed entertainment and butchered language

The elders grow weaker physically, remaining mentally sharp
to witness all that they and their forefathers built erased from
recorded history

Wretched

Barbarians at the gates

Barbarians breach the gates

Barbarians construct new gates

Looking for the next cause to consolidate their antagonism

Moving through cycles of thuggery and thievery

Proud of their effervescent plundering

You cannot leave

The gates close

Your life is over

Centuries of bloodthirsty bandits smile over your coffin

Shared Purpose

I can still hear the audience cheering in the movie theater

A momentous moment in a classic movie

The hero overcomes the villain

Good triumphs over evil

The crowd embraces the commonality for what they hope transpires

Then, new stories replace the old… slicker than the old

Films with great nuance and complexity, so they say

In reality, one-dimensional and uninspiring

Purposely produced with bad purpose

The audience cheers less and less

Shared purpose turns to a fractured crowd

Commonalities turn to unalterable differences

Outside of the movie theaters

Cohesion turns to tribalism

Did They Die in Vain?

Has it all been for nothing?

Did the Revolutionary War dead revolt in vain?

Did the hundreds of thousands of Civil War casualties die in vain?

Did those that fought segregation with mind, body, and spirit fight in vain?

Did the men who defeated socialist empires emerge victorious in vain?

Have all the arts, sciences, and advancements in human history to this point all occurred for nought?

The cynically infused cultural self-doubt became palpable, and the taste of the self-doubt, nauseating

If a powerful culture spoils and rots on the vine, the firmly rooted tree of civilization decomposes

Civilizational death would render unparalleled historical importance

To those that toiled and sacrificed for a brighter future

The sacrifices of great men will never be in vain

The actions of societal murderers will be in vain... after we're long gone

Perish

It all unravels thread by thread

Evil rituals trample and replace rich traditions

Universities become insane asylums

Entertainment becomes naked perversion

Business becomes ideological

Science becomes stifled by medical witchcraft and pharmaceutical sorcery

Families break apart

Friendships fracture

Your neighbors muzzle themselves

Prices skyrocket

Value vaporizes

Values burn and the embers of life drift away in the night

You wake up and wonder whether your nightmare was real

And if indeed you are still alive

Or went straight to the scorching realm of the trident-wielding destroyer

The Positivity Delusion

Use positivity to deceive ourselves and others

Apply positivity's magic tricks to enable artificial success and superficial happiness

Bask in positivity to keep ourselves wrapped in illusions of personal stardom

Embrace positivity to control the thoughts and actions of others around us

Drink barrels of positivity... addictive concoctions poisoning our visions and distorting our purposes

Positivity, the son of pride and the devious fraternal twin of the equally devious negativity

Positivity of our own conjuring

Not the natural wellspring of energy granted to us throughout our lives

Castles

Cleaning your room is part of a multi-pronged strategy to defend your castle

But when the arrows barrage your sanctuary

Protect your fortress

Otherwise you will not have any rooms still standing to clean

Clarity

Left the rage

And all debilitating emotions

Far behind

The rearview mirror

Steady Rain in the Altered Atmosphere

The steady rain yields the most problems

What you are experiencing is the reality of a changed environment

The air is thinner

Storms increasingly intense

The ground, less stable and prone to destructive seismic activity

Breathing is more laborious than ever

Though you did not construct these current environs of civilization

Needing to adapt is a reality hoisted upon you and everyone else

The deliberately harmful terraforming has changed the weather patterns

Thus changing protection measures that would assure your balance over the ground you walk

And would assure your balance with the elements you endure

This is the same for all of us

Despite the geographic and atmospheric difficulties

Most of the time it is just steady rain

How can you reconfigure the wider environment and earth on your own?

You cannot, and you know this already

In laboring to do so, you unnecessarily risk becoming a self-perceived god

At constant battle with other gods

You cannot control the harsh weather or seismic shifts and eruptions

But you can shield yourself from the driving rain

You can wear oxygen tanks

You can find the vehicles to hover above ground during the quakes and lava flows

Just remember as you wear your rain gear

Others still get drenched and swamped by the driving rain

Sometimes they do not have the arks to ride out the floods

It is a gargantuan undertaking to build an ark that fits people
outside of your family

When you see someone soaked by the rain and sleet and hail

You can always give them an umbrella or help them find shelter

I know you will weather the current storm and the cumulonim-
bus clouds will dissipate

You and your family will be safe

Someday, the old atmosphere might even reappear

In the meantime, amid atmospheric upheaval, you can help
people deal with the driving rain

The future depends on it

Leave Your Village

The need to uproot has been true since before Abraham left Ur

Since before Noah built the ark

Since Adam and Eve left the Garden

No choice but to leave old villages, real and virtual

Sometimes you can go back

Sometimes you cannot

People's mocking and dismissiveness keep you imprisoned

You have the key to unlock your own cell

You owe no explanations other than to your Creator

Your hesitations obey the notions others have for you

Let those notions go, and often times, let those people go

Or understand that at some point, the judge and juries change
as well

Regardless, let your hesitations drown in their fears

Let your fears drown in the hesitations of the old village

Pressure

An ever expansive push to conform

Peer pressure's influx waxes and wanes

The begrudging acceptance of following the worst that people
and convention offer

The balloon of conformists' actions pops

Releases the trapped air

A loud sound and nothing more

The conformists' exasperation oscillates

Their opportunity to ramshackle you disappears

Vision Restored

Shades of emptiness and jaded memories

Larry stands at the edge of the world and looks across the vista of his life

The 94-year-old's vision restores with only moments left

Some of his victims still walk through a maze of his minefields

His sins pay homage to nobody in return for his followers' crazed allegiance

Larry is too old for the self-imposed emptiness of vacuous celebrations

He always was

After eons of wasted time and efforts

Larry's eyes close, and they never open again

Here's to a New Marriage

A good friend got married

A man and a woman under God, united in a clear vision of sacrifice

I watched with joy as my friend embarked on his next odyssey in life and manhood

All during the reception, I realized that never have I attended a wedding ceremony so heartfelt and meaningful

My friend and his bride restored added hope for my view of mankind

A broken species, always looking to rebuild, reformulate, and reinvent

Few expeditions more meaningful than the ancient unison of marriage

Here's to my friend and his new bride

May their days be long, healthy, and purposeful

And may the same of be true for all

The Festival

The wind picks up as the sun drops

Beautiful atmosphere with people walking the long row of vendors

Cannolis to meatball submarines

Pizza to sausage and peppers

A season finale of food trucks and charities, rides and bands, sightseers and locals

An array of smiling, dancing, and eating

Men and women in mini-parades, marching in short processionals to the onlookers' delight

Instrumentalists playing old-time tunes

A place for the young and the old

Singles and couples

Families and friends

People walking the streets, carefree

Restaurateurs working a long holiday weekend with grace, good cheer, and passion

Every bite of food has value

A priceless October festival

The crowd does not disappoint

Gentle zingers back and forth

A happy feeling to celebrate and enjoy the cool sea air

New explorations beckon

Full moon appears, its light dimmed by passing clouds

A memorable day and night of Columbus

Vampire Bat

The crushing weight of my solitude fractures into easily swept up emotional debris

I, a vampire bat, let in the sunlight

The radiance jams my sonar

Reverting to human form to navigate across an atmosphere showered by the star's brightness

Ghosts from the Living Past

Robert faces a constant barrage of turmoil from the past

His ghosts jeer at him to slide into oblivion

A booming chorus of spirits to pull him backward in time

A crescendo of haunting melodies threatens his tenuous sanity

He knows a break from sanity would kill any remaining flicker inside to keep living.

With the past still alive, Robert holds fast to the decency of the past and present

He carries any particle of meaning forward to shield him against the ghosts that claw at his soul

Particles of meaning reveal themselves as waves of meaning

Wave energy becomes a force field to shock ghosts into knowing their rightful place

The ghosts bring messages as needed for Robert to remember his horrific deeds

He keeps them from wrenching him apart

His ghosts, from the living past, learn to respect the power of the breathing present

They join forces with Robert to follow the path laid out for him to the burgeoning future

Render to Whom?

Granting to Caesar what is God's

As though Caesar is a god

Nothing left of value to deliver

Sacrificing spirits for tyrants

Caesar renders unto us the promise of scorn, lies, deception, and
circuses

Promises that would force decadent kings of old to blush while
standing naked in the Garden

Desolate

You find yourself in a remote desert outpost

Find a way to greener lands

Or terraform your environment

Enrich the ground

Seed the clouds

Plant trees

Divert waters to your own reservoir

Don't steal the nutrients or riches

See what you have

See what you can produce

Stay above ground

Defeated

Some men hear no music in life

Other than the chords and drum lines of futility

Bad Dreams

Illusory trophies

Mutiny yields timidity

Golden calves dominate the proud

Academic

Intellectual exercises stir up

Perpetual self-doubt disguised as

Confidence that gets

Devastated every day

What Do You See?

They prove themselves to be mirrors

Reflecting your own arrogance and deceit

Keep the Party Going

It's true Kenny likes to enjoy life

He just doesn't want to get drunk off of it

For feasts and celebrations, you might see him having a good time

You might see him observing the events unfolding before him

You might not see him at all

No need to break up the party on Kenny's account

Don't expect him to join it either

He's a mere mortal ghost passing through… and a sober one at that

Drunk

Drunk on malignant rumors

Gossip spreading the tumors

Heavyhearted sense of humors

Lost causes, Boomers to Zoomers

Passengers

All of us passengers on the ship of time

We have what we need and we have enough lime

Journeying through obstacles from birth to death

Winds pick up and we feel the ocean's breath

We tumble ashore each waking day at dawn

To find meaning beyond watering our lawn

Back to the pelagic with eyes dilating

Passed cliffs and trenches, our futures awaiting

Toast for Family

Family

A sturdy ship on the sea of life

Only God is more important

Only He can guide the sturdy ship to safe harbor

The Big Game

What happens after the big game?

Nothing earthly can last every season of every year

We follow myriad additional traditions

The sun still rises in the east and shines beyond the times of the pigskin

Traditions Crumble

Independence Day becomes July 4th

MLK Day devolves into segregated levels of purpose

Presidents' Day homogenizes Washington and Lincoln's birth-days

Thanksgiving transforms into the obese worship of avian demigods

Evil Eyes

Society descends one nonsensical moment at a time

Lustful auras mistaken for charm

Charm mistaken for prayer

Prayer to a would-be goddess worshipping a god

A god that sacrifices pieces of himself to gain her jealous loyalty

Woman meets a man with eyes more devious than the flames of deception that scorch his victims

Willing victims with unquenchable pride

As unquenchable as the animalistic man himself

The woman becomes another in a long line of victims

She believes she conquers the man with her energy, but she does not

The man claims his prize

The woman uses whatever sorcery she can to remain his prize

But the man has other presents to unwrap

He captures this woman as he does all of them

With the charm of a werewolf

She mistakes this for a game worth playing

A game that winds up in her chewed up spirit left for snow vultures on the glacier of lost souls

JOURNEYS REDUX (POEMS VI)

The Ides of Life

March 15th approaches

Sky blooms and the landscape peels off the winter frost

The mind becomes infused with the warmth of life

Faith survives within the heavy-handed bedlam and frenzied order

Surroundings that confound the best of us

Optimism in action to under ride and underwrite the yearly unveiling of spring

A portal to a better life

Seekers of hope reminded they need not suffer the fates of

tyrants or betrayers

Welcome to the dimension of purpose beyond happiness

Riding the crest of life to the afterlife

Performative

All social media's a stage

Mechanical acting

Vacuous curtain calls

Productions unworthy of individual and communal folklore

Speak

Speak your mind and pay the price

Shut your mind and force us all to pay forever

Spawning

From miserable friend springs miserable self

Additive

Lament alone

Aspire with many

Banana Democracy

"Save democracy and climate!" cry the tyrants from within the chambers of polluted souls

True Love

I love him, as long as he keeps his job

Consequences

He can have almost anything he wants... his casket awaits him and his horns grow faster than his nails

Lost Brothers

Friends are friends until they aren't

Then, they never were

Devotion

Beyond the shattered bonds... friendships fused in devotion

Unbalanced

Nice is too much... and never enough

Manhood

A boy stands tall amid the wreckage of a town he holds dear

Supposed men take the meandering cowardly roads through their own minds

Content to save themselves and hide in fear

They watch from a distance as the demons descend

The wicked and possessed attempt to crucify the boy upside down

All they know is how to inflict horror

The ignorant and evil rush to defend the indefensible

The boy perseveres, surviving the physical and emotional anguish the living dead unleash on him

As the "decent" onlookers regress back to childhood, the boy continues to manhood

He moves forward despite jeering from all those living quiet
lives of degradation

Trapped on a Prehistoric Dance Floor

The thirty, forty, and fifty-something women move out of
rhythm

Out of rhythm to the rap of the late 80s and early 90s

Once youthful appearances sapped out of drained faces

Drunken smiles turn to drunken frowns

Spastic in the high heels

Imitating a manic, wannabe trapeze artist

Moving as desperate dinosaurs across the lonely flashing lights

Married women with wondering eyes that cry out for the atten-
tion of fallen men

Band stops

DJ goes home

The memories of oblivion continue weekend after weekend

The Wild

Jim spent 14 years in the wild after Jessica left him

Fourteen years of wandering through the spiritual desert

Demonic cactuses poked him with their needles

Ghoulish coyotes howled frantically, while the sun would set as fast as it rose

Torrents of light rained down and guided Jim out of the desert

He entered a lush ecosystem with steady terrain

Traversed the soft grass and saw the sun remain in the sky

Jim's days of wandering were no more

Beyond the Pale

Wraiths concealing wrath behind bewildered and bewildering eyes

Filled to the brim with animus

Overflowing the peaks and valleys

Personas drenched in the flames of envy

Country Fried Diner

Not just out of any old film

The setting for many films

From many time periods

Rural décor

Country music

Happy faces young and old

Couples and families

Friends and acquaintances

Eggs and burgers on the tables

Ketchup and coffee on the counter

Welcome to the country fried diner

Visit us again real soon

We'd love to have you back

See you again in the movies

See you again in real life

See you again in your dreams

Permafrost

As warm as can be

Fleeting harmony

Wisp of pleasant dream

You choose the wrong team

Awaken to frost

Planet now lost

Tarred without feathers

Stranded forever

Hot and Cold

Flames of icicles and deception

Inescapable predilection

Evergreen desires still fester

Ready to burn the star-crossed jester

No Permission Required

I embarked on a spiritual journey across the United States

The angels provided me a map

Heading from New Jersey to California

I stopped in Ohio and asked jealous road warriors for permission to continue

Though not an angel that led me

I followed a different winged-creature down to perdition

Crossing

Crossed the Smokies, Mississippi, and Rockies at age ten

Traversed the Atlantic to the Pacific and back again

Inner battles through the decades lurked with glee

Only the creator of Heaven and Earth could set me free

Persevere

The great confusion wreaks misery upon millions

He keeps his patience and resolve

Pathways emerge

Destinations unfold

Roadblocks compel circuitous routes

A society in turmoil cannot plunge him into a craven life

For that would embroil him in death

How does anyone survive the trek through a civilization that loses its way?

Communities in shambles

Families in disarray

The lost spirit of the individual

Succumbing to barbarous vacuity

Dwelling in lost time

Seeking an existence within the canopy

A steady vision turns murky

Friends scatter

Family flocks away

Neighbors hiss

Enemies encircle

He conquers one phase of troubles to discover a clearing into the next

Arriving in the marshlands

Not the destination he longs to find

Yet the sunlight he longs to embrace

His march continues

A solitary march across the swamps and inlets, bays and bayous

A brackish journey for a brackish man

He seeks more than intertidal understanding

An opportunity to leave the estuary behind

Outlasting the sweat that disembowels any moment of comfort
or clarity

He moves through the desert

The sunlight develops an intensity he no longer clutches on his
face

He still favors the light and the oasis of flowers that greet him on
his quest

Terrain fraught with hardships and drudgery

Even in the desert roughness, shrubs and plants bloom as a
promise for defeating the obstacles

He makes his way along the edges of lazy waters

He stumbles upon racing rivers

Tributaries to oceans and lands far and wide

Waterfalls to liven his soul and jostle his urgency

An urgency mixing the need to move with the need to sit still

Recalibrating his mindset and maneuvers from one environ to the next

He wanders from one comatose community to the next

Discovering beauty everywhere amid the impenetrable wreckage

Back within the mountains

Natural pool of water covering the valley floor

Staring through the peaks and passed the low-lying clouds

The expedition must continue after a moment's rest

His lake in the valley a still frame to the following adventure

On to the tropics with fair winds dancing about the palm trees

He explores the lush landscapes from one island to the next

The sweltering seas turn to a cauldron of isolation

He pursues temperate atmospheres within... no matter if he finds them outside

Grass-fed hills lead him to and from discord

Traveling from high ground to low

Scouting for savannas

Finding them, but compelled to carry on with his voyage

He reaches the pinnacle of his journey

Winds his way down to the ocean

Translucent skies shower him from above

His odyssey advances through a broken civilization

An odyssey that proceeds within a man

A man letting his Creator perfect him amid permanent societal demise

Eels to Dolphins

From the deepest depths

Creatures of darkness beckon you

From the quiet and isolation

You swim through the long expanse

Searching for animated life

Whale sounds in the distance

Sharks circling in the open ocean

Finned predators create a perimeter around you

A light blinds their senses

You swim toward the friendly sounds

Warmhearted creatures and fellow mammals

Whales and dolphins jumping and playing

They welcome you to a magical realm

You just found your new home

Vampires

She presses on with the search to find herself

Looks to make up for lost time...

Lost in the deep forest of her mind

Walks upon a web of spirits that trap her for her next arachnid boyfriend

Untangle now!

Close call

Next, from her mind's sea canyons, an eel of a man approaches her

The moray male uses his zealously empty eyes to engage her

Escape!

Another close call

Now floats along her mind's abyssal plain

The light rays all but dissipate this far below the surface

Excuses to find herself amid wretched ecosystems

Biomes where women who damn the light cannot survive the beastly radiation of vampires

Basketball Player

Derrick always enjoyed the innocent kind of fun for which people despised him

He played basketball alone, when friends went to parties

He went to movie theaters alone, when friends went to raves

He dined alone on Friday nights, while his coworkers drank themselves into blackouts

Derrick, a loser as defined by many who knew him

Sometimes Derrick agreed he was indeed a loser

Then he would remember he never liked the nights out with those addicted to sleazy fun

They mocked him for wanting to just play and appreciate simple pastimes

Such is the life of Derrick

Never a partier

Just a basketball player, who most of the time knows who he is

And who always knows who he never wants to be

Intrepid

Heavy countenance

He stumbles forward

Weakened senses

Stifled coordination

Desperate for his powers to return

An opaque veil of despair to muddles his surroundings

Lodging in the realm of perplexity

Walking the maze of lost legends

Locked in a labyrinth of descending ghouls

Converging on his fading life

But all of a sudden

Electrified by a flash

Magnetized by burgeoning currents

The crumbling labyrinth scatters the ghouls back to their wicked realms

Dispersing foes with an angelic power not of his own creation

His weakness falls away through a portal he does not enter

Another portal opens before him

His path to the future unfolds atop the wreckage of the maze he conquered

He crosses the threshold

Another labyrinth appears

Ready to unleash the intrepid angels

Stripped

Forced isolation keeps me entombed in perpetual sleep

Mummified and deprived of light and nourishment

Layers of wickedness spiral around me

Every hour wraps me in place as I grow desperate

While one season crashes through the next

Nowhere to turn and nothing to provide solace

I begin the quest to unwrap myself from the torment of imposed confinement

Rebellious action against the evil forces on a mission to mummify humanity

My consciousness moves from a trance to the brink of sovereignty

Layers of my encasing unravel as the wicked forces scream in panic

Stripped of outer coverings and escaping the embalmer

I have the clothes on my back

A refreshed mind in my head

Awake and free from mummification

I stand ready to help humanity unsheathe itself from forced isolation

Foreboding gives way to purpose in the age of focused rebellion

Citadel on Fire

Republic to oligarchy to embers

Trajectory of a society unwilling to remember it did not create the Heavens and the Earth

Entering the phase of embers

We live amidst the explosive flames that scorch our culture with third-degree burns

Disfigured and writhing in pain

Civilization has nowhere to recover from the arson attack it endures

Nothing remains of our citadel but the smoldering we cannot stop

The spiritual architecture of a once great land burns into fading memory

The ashes disperse through the seven seas

No republic

No oligarchy

Just embers

Zealots

High priests of shame

Keep people silent

Force obedience

Mandate suffering

Punish the supposedly sinful

Ascribe human flaws to Western civilization

Claim suppressive ethnic and racial DNA

Shame into subservience

Impress group salvation upon all

Project rage and inadequacy onto non-adherents

Cast off those who dare not follow the scam artists of collective shame

Tribal Apparitions

The purported oppressed of today spawn the oppressors of tomorrow

Tribalism conquers any notion of rising above

Future victims yet to walk the planet

Their ghosts haunt our descendants' destinies

Smoke

Firefighting for countless years in the forests of poisonous ideologies

Asphyxiated by overwhelming fumes in the societal tinderbox

Escape Pod

The desolate hellscape made its home in the minds of millions

Trapped inside mental prisons with no keys for release

The fortunate escaped their mental anguish before the isolation consumed them

They discovered fields, streets, and homes of respite and replenishment

Launched beyond the heavy atmosphere when others could not

Rocketed away from the desolate hellscape

The Great Excavation

Stripped bare of all spirit

Today's man hovers over a fire of trepidation

Submit to every whim of those who dangle the spoiled carrots

Conformity-enforcing rabbits ingest the carrots as you approach

Rabbits pulled from the hats of wicked magicians

The nonconformist arises

Railing against the life impressed on him

Live and breathe to strike against the docile nature of the obedient

A frustrated follower or an unconventional outcast?

Oscillate between two roads of extinction

New earth solidified underneath and stretched out for further than the eye can see

The eager explorer with a reliable map and compass

Trekking along the crystallized pathway

The gauntlet appears and flummoxes the discoverer

Plummets through the fractured, once firm ground

The great excavation begins

Unearthing him and restoring the precarious environs he took for granted

Up from the mantle and back on firm land

Small fissures in the crust remind him of the porous depths of failures past

Descendants could still vaporize in the heat of cultural on-
slaughts of the future

Agony Abates

Banished from your peer group and alone with your thoughts

Vanished from your usual social events

Vanquished by an all-consuming and decrepit culture

Your spirit swims in the high tide of frustration

This high tide no longer ebbs and flows

You face a continual high tide and its concomitant currents

Pummeled and transported against your control to the roughest
of waters

The wardens of your spirit gained strength at the behest of your
fears

Buried in the mud of a presently infertile civilization

What a pox upon humanity to watch societal wildebeests de-
vour cultural marvels

You watch the devouring and internalize your own powerless-
ness to stop it

A weakness you harvest while you swallow your tongue

Would your beleaguered acceptance of defeat smother all the smoldering flames inside you?

Or would beleaguered acceptance fan a raging fire to consume you?

Sprouts of courage mature from within

The high tide of frustration ebbs

Fortunate timing brings your spirit cast adrift back to shore

Silence to Renewal

You cannot speak freely anywhere

Not in public or in private

Not jokingly or seriously

Muzzle your voice and your family's voices

Muzzle your thoughts and actions

And your family's thoughts and actions

You dare not speak with conviction

Lest you find those who use your conviction to destroy you

You speak with the living demons

Knowing not why they fall under spells

Spells of culture-twisting, contortionists and alchemists

The typical bonds that link mankind continue to disappear

Frayed bonds, later decimated

You now live in a cosmic dust bowl of isolation

Removed from much of society

Removed for much of yourself

The fragments and debris scattered throughout the
drought-laden land of your life

Tumbleweeds of despair swirl in the harrowing winds

Small yet lasting cuts from the jumping cactus of your mind

What lies beyond this desert that leaves you thirsting for a vast
reservoir of civilization?

Your faith, renewed among the sand-swept plains and hills

Renewed despite all those lost in the desert, transfixed by spells
from sun-soaked serpents

COLD CUTS (VIGNETTES I)

Sunlight Glowing in the Madness

Steve lived to tell about it. Waves crashed gently over his face as the previous lifetime shifted into focus. The old crew moved on, the tired habits withered, and a new energy rocketed through the town. Sorrow turned to vigor. The flood of courage drowned all the fires of psychosis, and the sea mist carried the promise of a future that evaporated the town's recent lunacy.

Alphas and Betas

George blazed his own path. He saw both the aggressive and submissive as rotten from the inside out, made in their own image out of the recipes from a prix fixe personality menu. The alphas and betas enforced their expectations on those who want no part in relationships built on houses of marshmallows. Clear-sighted, George discovered the wreckage in his life from all the aggressive and submissive. The friends that never were. The romantic interests that could never be. Life got better. But the question still haunted him... "What now?"

From Sky to Bog

My guardian angel protects me every day. I sense her energy as she stands by my side. One with the afterlife, she clearly sees my fallen nature, and she knew of it also during her physical time on Earth. The women since have almost destroyed me... almost... but unsuccessful, and so life continues in search of a woman I can call my wifely companion on this blue, disheveled, beautiful planet. Perhaps my guardian angel will help me draw her from the crowd as Arthur drew Excalibur from the stone.

The Last

Jimmy lay dying beneath the planetarium of the night sky. Friendless, rudderless, and empty... except for the last gasp of sincere regret that kept him alive long enough to remember how he entered the world... just a person, dreams later born and shattered. He approached the end of his time on Earth, while his companion stared into the distance. Starlight flickered across the horizon as Jimmy closed his eyes for the last time.

Sight

Alexander punctured his destiny with needles of conformity. His misdeeds altered his life's trajectory to a meek existence. Sitting atop the dawn sky's precipice, hope reigned as his guardian angel woke him yet again. Alexander lost many years since his sight disappeared to the nightmares of his choosing. He brushed off the cobwebs from his mind. No more nightmares and no more conformities. Recognizing the damage he inflicted, his destiny's wounds healed and his sight returned. He would never welcome nightmares again.

The Desperate Quest

Joseph became a lost adventurer on the road to somewhere redundant. Always on the move, he could not find the old world in which he thrived.

The world of treasure-seeking, beauty-seeking, and purpose-seeking disappeared from under Joseph's feet. He stayed on the go to avoid watching everything crumble around him. Joseph hoped the fresh faces and geography would bring solace to his beleaguered mind. His peace of mind had already sublimated without notice or concern from those whose beleaguered minds trapped them in time, sloth, and mistrust. Yet the adventurer was not dead. Joseph knew his quest had many future memories to unveil. Would the sights and sounds of wrecked faces and abandoned towns obliterate his will? Would the noise of the crowded eateries and meetups ring increasingly hollow from one day to the next?

Joseph's fate teetered on the brink of the worthiness of his quest... and on the destiny of the grounds he traversed... a destiny out of his control.

Downswing

Ron experienced emotional carnage in solitude.

He stayed home to avoid the same scavengers feasting on his soul month after month, year after year...

Ron knew he had to venture back out into the world.

Unconvinced he learned his lessons for handling the trials awaiting him, he would keep himself isolated within the four walls of an apartment he grew to detest.

Neither television nor phone nor music would bring him comfort.

Ron's feelings of a doomed fate inundated his apartment.

Upswing

Ron felt his mind slide past the breaking point of dealing with the trials that awaited him.

His fears entangled him as he writhed in still and silent anguish.

Laying in the darkness, ambient light seeped through the windows, and he saw the contours of his four apartment walls.

He recognized that nothing terrifying existed beyond or within the walls.

Ron anticipated trials that would never come to fruition.

The real trials revealed themselves as ongoing inside this frightened man.

Would he now embrace the trials?

His heart smiled as he discovered he could let go of his terrors and leave the confines of his four-walled apartment.

The Reluctant Dragon

Zilgore approaches the mountainous metropolis with hesitation.

For years he soars from system to system, decimating cities with rivers of heat from his mouth.

This time he reflects on what such a city at altitude, unharmed, can mean for him.

A new home could await if he leaves the metropolis intact and forages in the valleys.

Zilgore knows now that he ages with every passing attack, and his wings tire from the battles.

The reluctant dragon lands on a recently thawed hilltop for yet another scorched-earth assault.

Deluded Super Alpha

Kenny fancied himself an untouchable.

Not born into wealth, he scratched and clawed for all he gained.

What he desired became his.

In his mind, he earned the right to the community's praise.

Fulfillment eluded him.

He saw an opportunity in Allison to gain satisfaction from her if she endlessly sacrificed for him.

To win her, he would have to become a thief.

He knew it would be easy to steal... he was already a god.

Sacrificing Abel

Jerry became the object of people's intense derision.

They mistreated him with an emotional brutality.

His wife sacrificed him for a man with power and money.

A group of Jerry's friends sacrificed him to social climb.

His coworkers sacrificed him for professional accolades.

Jerry was simply part of the continuation of these people's long lines of sacrifices.

Eventually, they would have nothing to sacrifice but their entire souls.

Their offerings appease nobody, and Jerry survives the onslaughts of life with the same genuine spirit found in Adam's second son.

Lifted Curse

Our hero rejoices in lighthearted banter with the friendly waitress.

That's all it takes.

And the remnants of a demon queen's seven-year curse continue to fracture.

The old spell has no power anymore to affect the mood of our hero.

The curse, thought to be a juggernaut, breaks into millions of pieces, swept away by one woman's kindness.

Curses of the demon queen drive men to the brink of madness and beyond it.

Our hero survives the old spell and never enters the demon

queen's lair.

The curse fizzles into nothing as our hero, without fear, courts the friendly waitress.

Almost Was... Always Is

The woman running the diner was tired. Not physically exhausted, but emotionally spent.

Things became difficult. It got tougher to hire reliable staff. The rent price went up. Old friends and old flames moved away... some moved so far away that they moved into the afterworld.

She keeps their thoughts and memories alive. The tributes in pictures of her parents and grandparents, scattered across the diner with their smiles attached to the determined grit of their faces.

With no children, and nieces and nephews far away, the diner is all she has left. It keeps her going. She feeds people and always will. A little rough around the edges, just one morning in her presence at the restaurant reminds us that in our own ways, we can all be a little rough around the edges.

The woman running the diner was almost a wife and mother. But she will always be a daughter, granddaughter, a niece, an aunt, a cousin, a woman, and a human being. And as long as she's alive, she'll see to it that nobody around her goes hungry.

Ribeye Sandwich and Fries

I must continue my drive up the shore to the celebrations. My goal, one festivity after another on this Saturday evening of Thanksgiving weekend. The scene up the shore, where I can spread my wings, dine on overpriced food, and spend time with overpriced people. I can consume the alcohol slowly and let a steady buzz take me through the wee hours of Sunday morning. This is going to be one great night.

I cannot determine what else to do with myself to escape the clutch of a solitary life. Already a distance from home, I can enjoy the novelties of my first stop, in a quiet shoreline town, and I can avoid traveling to tempting locations of the Siren. The illusory faces of beautiful women flash before me. The women's mouths whisper, "You waste my time in an unexciting shore town." I look around in my present time and place, seeing calmness and the beginnings of Christmas cheer. I see people that are real. Nothing in this quiet town to veer me off course from staying true to myself. The string of one distraction after another... it must end tonight.

The quiet shore town creates a friction that grinds my vehicle to a crawl. I spot an eatery by the water as I slow down. Celebratory scene or not, I am hungry. I step inside and the atmosphere shields me from my desire to join the festive dwellers up the shoreline. I look around and realize I just want to be around fellow human beings. College football plays on the television as people enjoy the informal eatery, located off the beaten path. I have a scrumptious ribeye sandwich with delectable fries, bringing me back into balance.

A calm town and food show me the way back to harmony this late November Saturday at dusk. A ribeye sandwich and fries are all I need tonight. No time to waste on hollow meetups and shallow evenings. Though I just might talk to a few people here tonight. After all, they are real, living on this Earth beyond the confines of my phone's virtuoso performance of trapping me to my virtual connections.

Accepting Defeat

Jacob always seems to claw himself out of impossible situations. He never backs down, but this time looks different. The current scenario appears bleaker than anytime he can remember throughout the course of the past decade... His in-laws are visiting.

This is not just any other visit. This is Christmas weekend. Jacob dreads their visit every year, though especially this year. The in-laws have a special weapon in their arsenal. This year marks an extended visit until the New Year. Jacob has to deal with the constant barrage of questions about when he and his wife will have children. He has to deal with the snide remarks about his flailing career. He has to deal with the constant background noise of music he hates. Not simply for a weekend. Ten days of haranguing and sarcasm. Ten days of loud dishes in the sink in the early morning. Ten days of the television blasting through the walls and piercing Jacob's nervous system.

Jacob has a plan to drive the in-laws away early. He can announce he wants a divorce... except that he doesn't want one. He can leave town for a friend's for the weekend, except his wife would not allow it. He can invite his own parents over to drive out the in-laws, except the in-laws would stay out of spite. Every plan falls apart in Jacob's mind. By New Year's Eve, the end of the visit is in sight.

New Year's Eve at home. Jacob, his wife, and his in-laws. Just before 8 PM, he devises a new plan to set the house on fire, except that he remembers it's his home, and he does not want anyone to die. The clock strikes midnight and the in-laws decide to turn in for the night.

Jacob relishes that a brief victory is at hand. He has some time alone to enjoy a couple of hours with his wife before sleeping. His father-in-law cooks up some food and starts a grease fire. The alarm goes off and by the time Jacob gets down to the kitchen, the father-in-law just finishes using the fire extinguisher. Jacob finally accepts defeat. He may have lost this year. He is determined to win next year... but so are his in-laws.

Stuck

Another cold winter envelopes the Northeast, with frozen thoughts and memories of old hopes and promises. The clock forgot to wind itself. Years later, time remains solidified.

A society destroys itself with each passing month. Vitriol is so strong as to congeal around the hearts of the once carefree. Nothing moves forward. Everything stagnates or devolves.

In the recent past, one could find a cadence in life. One could modulate that cadence. One could self-correct. One could follow the road to a destiny without shackles of societal mania.

A shell-shocking frenzy continues its march to dominate the land. The frenzy is both loud and quiet, driving an invincible saber through every community. Cities, towns, and countryside mourn the freezing of time and the bitter cold hypothermia across a civilization suspended in hypnosis.

The rotting society moves toward permanent decay. A powerless people sink into tribal caves, establishing new dwelling places in the darkness until time regains fluidity and vitriol melts off the hearts of men.

Ancient Palace, Modern Castle

Experience the journey through unique but converging places. The journey resonates with the harmonic balance between man and the natural world.

An ancient palace thrives in the evergreen valley. The palace, constructed of bark and leaves, rocks and mud. Fresh rain arrives to grow the dwelling and clean the living rooms. Open-air living rooms showcase plants and flowers, branches and pebbles. The ancient palace dates back as far as geologic time itself, inhabited now and for countless eras by bear and elk, bobcats and chipmunks, coyotes and cardinals.

The river separates the ancient palace from the modern castle, less a moat than a link from one world to the next. Leaping trout and paddling crayfish populate the flowing citadel. The citadel, a nexus between the old and the new, the natural and the manmade. The river glides between an ancient palace and modern castle, winding through the mountains and off into the unknown. Bears of the palace visit the flowing citadel, much to the fishes' chagrin.

Modern manmade castle stands at the edge of geologic time. Moss and ferns cross the river from the ancient palace to the castle gates. Windswept pine needles form a shifting trail to the massive towers of stone. The courtyard entertains flying visitors from the palace. Magnanimous human beings permit long-term flying visitors to nest, allowing small and natural fortifications within the castle walls.

Distinct bastions link as one earthly fortification. A journey through time and space from the ancient palace to the modern castle.

If We Sing Loudly Enough

The crowd sings along with the old classic rock tunes at the pub. They cheer on the hired singer, who hears accolades from the crowd for the selection of hits he matches to his voice and acoustic guitar.

One request after another for the old sounds in rock that nobody produces anymore. The classics wither away as the middle-aged generation in the bar longs for a time long gone. Memories of movies, first dates, stylish cars, and a tough style of life. The singer's choices remind the middle-aged of their younger years. He reminds them of a time when their musical preferences influenced so much about entertainment and culture.

A pub audience with a hint of aggression more than of good cheer. Singing along more loudly with each hit, playing air guitars and air drums. To the middle-aged group, if the crowd sings loudly enough, the 1960s, 1970s, or 1980s could return. Transport awaits to take them from the Cape of Inebriation to the Island of Regression.

The crowd doesn't love classic rock the way the singer loves it. The crowd lusts after the music, and if the pubgoers sing loudly enough, the 60s, 70s, and 80s might take out a restraining order on the middle-aged bar heroes.

Starvation

Tommy is starving. Not food deprived. Not sleep deprived. Not shelter deprived or love deprived. He starves for a reinvigorated society. The old energy and hustle and bustle elude one city to the next, including his own.

Life continues as it has in the past across the great megalopolises... without the gusto. Tommy witnesses the lack of enthusiasm with every walk. He senses the emptiness with every one of his dying relationships. He experiences it with every robotic communication, emotional tirade, and passive-aggressive argument. He feels the callous attitudes with every quiet space in conversation. A cruelty found as well in the dismissive former friends. Former friends turned androids from hell. Tommy's hunger for a reinvigorated society does not return quickly. He must rest so as not to over expend limited energy slipping from his spirit. Tommy meets other starving people, and they search with him for all the evasive dynamism.

Tommy and his kindred spirits are not wizards. They are not magicians, sorcerers, mystics, or time travelers. They are not miracle workers. They are simply humans in search of a lost society. A lost society that presents itself before them, yet remains unreachable across current and future history. Though emaciated, Tommy loses his appetite while his quest disintegrates to roaming through a mind scape embroiled in oblivion.

Mythic

Brad risks it all to join the echelons of heroes from folklore. We hear about these men like Perseus. We imagine how they live, but so few of them do we meet in our own time. Brad shows us the genuine sacrifices of a hero. He gives up adventures in faraway lands to go on family vacations. He stops fighting monsters and finds an office job with a monster of a boss. He relinquishes brotherhood with kindred spirits, instead finding no common interests with coworkers and the sanitized friends his wife allows him to see. Brad quits on getting enshrined into historic tales of greatness... in return for career advancement. He becomes a legend at office parties and family reunions. He trades in fleeting mythical status to earn his destined mortality... a hero to his kids, and every now and again, a hero to his wife.

A Couple, Their Anniversary, and Their Son

Quiet town at the shoreline on a frigid Saturday afternoon in the dead of winter. A couple visits from an hour away to celebrate their anniversary. Together for decades, the husband and wife know each as well as any spouses can know each other, as they show by their conversation and demeanor. They enjoy the atmosphere at the restaurant overlooking the bay. I enjoy meeting them. It's what makes it even tougher to hear their story

We talk about subjects ranging from sports to boating to the Caribbean; I learn about their tragedy. I don't learn the details of their tragedy. No details other than their son's dying of an overdose three years ago. The three of us have an implied mutual understanding of the sickness in society that continues to destroy the lives of countless fellow citizens. A society that continues to dishonor the couple. I don't ask if they have any other children. These are decent people, and the focus should not shift away from the love they have for their deceased son.

The couple is jovial before the tragedy comes up in conversation. Unbeknownst to me at first, I lead the discussion to the past horror that time cannot heal for them. As I leave the restaurant, we exchange warmhearted goodbyes. As I look back, I see the man consoling his wife. They once again relive the nightmare of their son dying from poison. A poison streaming across the border with society-paralyzing intensity.

The couple is a casualty of the monsters. Monsters in offices we trust to protect the culture and our families from monsters on the street. Instead, the culture increasingly rots with the drugs and the violence. The culture rots with neglect and wanton encouragement of poisonous infiltrations. The culture rots and rots, revealing ongoing markers of rotting beyond the point of recognition. Into the abyss we all charge. Together we all barrel toward oblivion as a planetary train off its tracks in the cosmos.

I pray the couple finds peace in this world and the next. They look at me as though they know me. They have a look so familiar. The couple reminds me of an amalgamation of the best of family friends and kind strangers I meet throughout the years.

An all-too-common story of a young man dying before his time. A story of a young man, all too similar to the stories of too many other young men. But an individual. Not a number. An individual more than worthy of remembrance, and I will tell the story of him and his parents for the rest of my days.

Shopping in Bewilderment

It was everyone for themselves. Nobody was in anything to-
gether.

An elderly woman shopped amid the frenzied and the panicked.
I didn't help her at the first grocery store, but I did when I saw
her at the second. I guess we both scoured for various items we
couldn't find in one store. She was grateful for the help. I was
grateful to provide it in whatever way I could, especially after
not seizing the opportunity to help out the first time around.

Society marked itself with certifiable lunacy. An indelible mark
of the beast that we willingly accepted for less wealth than three
magic beans.

Soon I would not see the frenzied and panicked shoppers quite
as often. People retreated into their caves, heralding their tribes
at the expense of all other tribes and all other individuals. Not all
people did this, but finding out who was who became difficult
in a landscape littered with emptiness. The ghosts hid in caves
as well. The ghosts of conformity and phony fellowship of man.
Frenzy and panic gave way to scorn and banishment. A societal
concoction that killed the spirits of individuals and produced
incarnate ghosts from the encasings of a once vibrant people.

Here we stand three years later with emptier shelves at stores.
Here we stand three years later with emptier souls in life. Here
we stand destined for burial under mounds of societal dirt shov-
eled upon us by the beast we invited into our dismembered
civilization.

I wonder if the elderly woman escaped the surrounding lunacy. I wonder if she avoided the ongoing bewilderment society attempted to thrust on us all. I wonder if all the good-natured sacrifices she made in her life can ever melt the icy spirits of the people and powers that sought to whisk her away into the burial grounds of history.

A New Day

Gone. Finished. Dismantled.

The old ways dissipate and turn into spirit. A spirit formless and powerless to save the pride and possessions of a beleaguered people. The spirit promises to return, even while a new day presents itself before us. A new day glowing not in brightness, but glowing in the destruction of all things meaningful.

A new day with no redeeming qualities. Replacing the old without regard for any moment in history or future. A present riddled with intense worship of the newly followed gods. Gods envious of mere mortals. Mortals with no worth beyond what they can provide the gods. The mortals must sacrifice their words and thoughts and actions. They must sacrifice their minds and hearts and souls.

Sacrificed minds no longer hold or harvest the intuition needed by a floundering civilization. The inventive people disappear into a void of the systems the people construct. Ingenuity uncovered down the line within the hardened lava of a bygone civilization, excavated by our descendants. The descendants can excavate our ideas, yet never exhume our individual minds. Minds with dimming brilliance, yielding power to the gods that drink man's mental forces through a straw from Hell. Cerebral casings collapse into dust. Collapsing into dust at the hands of sorcerers on a rampage against humanity.

The gods demolish men's hearts. Hearts broken beyond repair as every chamber cries out helplessly for a mercy that never arrives. An earthly mercy that the gods cannot grant. Thieves of men's hearts, the gods pulverize the beating organ and all vessels pumping durability through men's lives. The gods sacrifice lives against the wills of the men still grasping to the notion that the old ways can return. Grasping to the notion that a once great civilization's banished spirit re-emerges victorious. A victory elusive to the men stripped of their hearts. Stripped of their hearts in the processing plants of covetous deities. Sacrificed hearts join sacrificed minds in the living underworld of the mindless and heartless.

Men's souls become the last bastion of a drowning culture. The last bastion loses strength by the moment. A strength unsalvageable during the ceremonies of final sacrifice. The gods yet again compel a sacrifice never wished or intended by the people now doomed and flooded for the rest of physical existence. When the final sacrifice ends, the last rebel breathes the rest of whatever breaths he has left. The gods win their battle. They win their war. They win their desire for a new day.

The new day cannot last forever. It does not last forever. The old ways return with the spirit that guides them. The spirit crushes the gods and the corruption of the new day. Men's minds, hearts, and souls reconstitute in the future generations. The gods took us as a sacrifice, but our descendants can live without the fears that ingest us. The new day is gone. A newer day arrives. Mankind can rejoice with hearty and humble spirit once again.

Shades

The dogmatic relativist finds an earthly absolution in his resolute stance to convert nonbelievers at the edge of a sword. He claims to the contrary that peace drives his beliefs and actions. Such a mangled vision of peace crumbles with every word spewing from his vile mouth... and every disfigured expression on his wretched face.

ILLUMINATION (VIGNETTES II)

Beyond the Casket

The funeral ends, and for many, the death of consciousness is just beginning. Not for Ben. Ben merely enters a state of deep confusion that feels like the end of his life. He now faces the first test of just what kind of life he seeks for himself and his remaining family.

Ben stares at the casket of his son, Paul. His son, only seven years old, had a smile that could cheer Ben up after the most dreadful days of work at a dead-end job. The casket appears to Ben as an illusion. He wonders if his son is actually inside. None of this seems possible. He sees Paul running up and down the street with friends a week ago. One week ago, alive and happy. The next week, in a casket and about to get lowered into the unforgiving Earth.

Seated at the funeral, surrounded by family and friends, he once again recounts his own existence. With laser precision he recounts the brief life of Paul. Paul, Ben's third of three boys, and the most joyful and carefree. Vivid snapshots and video of Paul's life flash before Ben's mind. He watches his little boy's first steps. He hears his first words and observes him playing, eating, growing, learning, questioning. Ben feels lifetimes of suffering coiled within his wilting spirit. He feels brutalized by the understanding that his son will never return in this life.

Joan, Ben's wife of twenty years, cannot stop wailing. Ben's companion through the rockiest of roller coasters and along the smoothest of highways. She does her best to maintain composure for her two living sons, but she cannot help letting loose the torment she feels. Ben feels his wife's agony. He does everything in his power to keep his crushed heart ticking, preventing the grief from pulverizing his sanity.

Mark and Eric hug their mother. They miss their little brother more than they can bear, and they sense a growing numbness mixing with their sadness. Ben observes his family and sits quietly. He has a wife and two sons, and for them his spirit must rebound.

Ben smiles in the middle of the funeral. He looks around, though nobody sees him. He smiles out of an ephemeral happiness amidst a terrifying reality. Ben envisions Paul's happiness, and this vision is not a product of Paul's imagination. Paul's spirit visits his dad in a moment of horrifying pain. Ben knows that his son's soul is alive, which allows Ben to find peace of mind to last him through the rest of his own time above ground.

Solace in a time of confusion and despair. Amid tragedy eclipsing the worst fears any parent could bear, Ben discovers the comfort that sustains him and his wife and children. He has the comfort of having had Paul in his and his family's lives, for however short a time it was. And he has a magnificent gift of having sons and a wife whose lives continue. Ben cherishes everything decent he has. He cherishes his past and what he has right before him. Ben reveres Paul's soul, a soul that endures after dirt and flowers cover the casket... a soul that endures forever...

There's Nobody Home

You travel to your hometown, but nobody greets you.

It's not out of rudeness. People at an old and still running pizza shop display friendliness rarely revealed or experienced elsewhere. More than a friendliness... a warmth and caring for community... a small area with thousands of people. Not a contrived caring or obligatory smile, it is a genuine warmth entrenched for decades despite the town's toughness. Maybe it is a former toughness. After all, you have not been there for quite some time.

You reflect on the changes and similarities of the area as you look through the pizza shop window. You hear and see the train rocket through the town. At many times a soothing sight and sound from your home and elsewhere, with an air of hopeful mystery about its destination points. The approaching and trailing locomotive, breaking up the restless energy of the cold and dreary northern winters.

It's been over 20 years since you left. Yet now you find yourself in the past. Suddenly it is 30 years ago, and then 35 years ago, and then 25 years ago. Time fluctuates as you see people reminiscent of those you used to know. The old parks. The old houses. The old families, many gone. No familiar faces on the streets. Streets that seemed much bigger through your childlike but quickly jaded and jading eyes.

Though traveling back in time, you walk the avenue of your old house. The rickety but effective individual air conditioning units. The yard where you used to play Whiffle ball, stripped of the trees and vegetation that breathed life and character into that modest but sacred space. Middle school punks used to trample through that sacred space.

You wondered if the punks you just saw at the pizza place were as bad as the ones who plowed through your yard 40 years prior. The punks today seem to have the rough language, but less raw anger or manipulative tendencies than you or the peers from your youth. Then again, it is the end of summer, and September could bring with it the town's rough-and-tumble attitude of yesteryear.

Continue walking up the slight hill of your original home-town street. Memories flood you of neighbors, friends, fights. Recollections bring forth the ghosts you had forgotten. You remember you and your childhood friends bicycling down the sloped avenue back home from the school you detested.

You observe more ghosts as you drive past the park of your high school years. The ghosts elicit good, bad, and beyond ugly remembrances. You realize that your travel back to your hometown elicited the apparitions.

What of the real people and places you notice on the streets? Some remind you of times and places past, and keep you from reaching the time warp's escape velocity you do not yet want to reach. Restaurants, diners, a shutdown bank, a replaced martial arts studio, a music album store that no longer exists. All spirits in their own right. Your crushes, your crushers, your crushing. Spirits roam the town. They seek you as you seek them. Many of the ghosts you want to bury. You had best watch them and avoid embracing the ones that move about as loners, in groups, or as figments of your imagination, embodied in real people and places.

You talk briefly with one woman on your old block, just across the street from your old house. She exudes a hesitant friendliness. Hesitancy comes from the residual skepticism inbred in this often cynical and wary town of an earlier era. The reason you talk to her is not to seek warmth. It's making sense of a greater past and present that moves on without your acceptance or rejection. This woman replaces your old neighbors and your old house's owners' replace you.

You understand you are a ghost and a visitor to the graveyard of your own history. Somehow, a version of your present marches forward, but you must find it outside the alleys and hangouts and pizza shops in this suburban time warp. As you reach escape velocity, the woman's smile fades and you rediscover the here and now.

During your travel back in time, you traversed old neighborhoods by car and foot. When you stopped by old friends' and acquaintances' places, nobody was home. Nobody was home except for some ghosts of past fellowship, rancor, and town character and lack thereof. Ghosts, real and imagined, cannot reveal themselves beyond the lessons of what brings you a better today.

If you keep going back and knocking on locked doors, you'll find nobody home.

Your family moved.

Your friends moved.

Your adversaries moved.

You moved.

Nobody's home, but you can always hear the train in the distance, moving across the backdrop of the past.

Nearing Obliteration

We look out across an endless field of spiritual corpses. Interplanetary enslavement, this measure serves as a microscopic objective of a much larger vision. Our vision is to ensure the irreversible and infinite death of souls, assaulting any of the facades which men clasp with all their might.

The spirit hunting begins by destroying the interplanetary customs and traditions to which mankind grows accustomed, such as eating and protection from the elements. Food and shelter remain in control of the interplanetary ruling body. With provisions needed throughout the colonies, we cannot tolerate selfishness on Earth to distribute all provisions as it sees fit based on myopic continental desires. We ship materials and nutrients where we decide, and when we decide.

We coerce the interplanetary populations by force to accept the rulings we codify. Food types and flavors must conform to our preferences. We respond to discrepancies meant to show originality by offering imprisonment or death in return. Surplus food production, cultivation, and unauthorized trade results in us confiscating food. Unapproved success ensures our enslaving perpetrators on their own lands, unless we remove them from their lands entirely.

We do not grant people the ability to travel or meet or talk with neighbors, except for approved activities and conversations. Flouting of the rules brings punishment of death to the willful perpetrators of individual spirit. People talk in person under the assumption that breaking our laws jeopardizes their lives and the lives of their families. They must all remain within their towns and villages.

Relics of old civilizations must die a painful death... as painful as the deaths, and lives, of the breathing creatures themselves.

Giving Away

Can Fred continue the charade of security in his profession while his spirit dies? He has payments to make. Payments on top of payments. Food... Mortgage... Vehicle... Luxuries... Yet what he fears more than losing his job is losing his social status. He knows he can keep both, but only if he risks the irreversible obliteration of his soul.

Fred stays in his job, lying to himself that he can help and be one of the good guys.

He lies to himself that he can stand up for his unjustly treated fellow professionals. All Fred does is lie to himself and the family he pretends he protects. Fred is scared and lazy. He asks for your understanding about his apathy. How can a man be trusted when he sacrifices his spirit for his status? He cannot.

And so Fred joins the long line in history of most men. Every now and again his energy and purpose bubble to the surface. Just as quickly, his energy and purpose dissolve into extinction.

You Are Where You Belong

You live in the era of wandering souls, yet you question why you feel misplaced. Your energy field reveals that you long for a home occupying a different space in history. What have you found but a convenient way you found to avoid digesting the failures of your own making? You have no mechanism or structure to absorb the time decay that threatens your heartbeat.

All your journeys bring you to the same location beyond reality. You find a region of dilated time that vaporizes your nightly dreams every morning. The morning turns to liquid futility. Desperation reigns and rains across the tundra of your energy field, freezing your ambition by late afternoon. Your desperate journeys collect the runoff from your glacial spirit.

You have nowhere else to live but in the now, puzzled about your era interfering with your energy field. The energy field loses power from the delusion that you can live in another time and space. Never need the evils of your era eclipse your awareness that the modern day remains your home... and where you belong.

Dining While the Floor Disappears

The ground falls out from beneath us, yet we continue vacationing. We continue with elaborate dinners. We go on acting as though the party never ends, and that the party is the point of everything. While the ground quakes, we become too inebriated by our passions to notice the point when the floor disappears. Nobody notices the clock strike midnight.

Never enough food and never enough wine. Let's go here and let's go there. Damn the torpedoes... full insanity ahead! We revel in spending and spending, not for needs or wants. We spend as part of the gravitational push and pull toward bankruptcy. Bankrupt souls try to sustain themselves on overpriced people, places, and events.

A society ingratiates itself with the perception that it can never falter. We encourage our pride born from generations of technological wizardry. Our wizardry reveals itself as not being bent on using advancements to propel mankind forward, but on being bent to the egos of people seeking to destroy everyone's spirit. With no ground on which to stand, society crashes through the crust and sinks to the mantle. We gaze at the narrowing sky as we fall with no landing. The sky vanishes from sight and the mantle of time boils us under the infernal crust of self-righteous vanity.

We dance from one night to the next. We celebrate and pretend all is well. None of our imaginations can will away the madness enveloping a culture breathing its dying breaths. The most expensive meal at the most expensive restaurant can bring no lasting joy. The cheapest meal at the cheapest sandwich shop can bring no peace of mind. All that remains is the inevitable descent into bedlam.

The floor cracks, and the ground gives way. The empty eateries sell their tablecloths and fine silverware for personal dietary needs. We seek scant food reserves and morsels of savings amid an energy scarcity apocalypse. Humanity screams into the future. Western civilization sinks for eons until reaching its final resting place of historical extermination.

Affliction

Murderous thieves afflicted us all. Insanity replaced normality. Everything stopped, suddenly and harshly.

How can the average man cope with such powerful changes?

One by one, the things man relied on for decades, even centuries, turned upside down.

Nowhere to go when places closed down. People kept friends at arm's length... at several arms' length, at the very least.

As the front-stabbing social climbers feared getting sick, they ostracized their other friends. At that point, where could a man go to interact with people close to him? The answer.... nowhere. He could go nowhere other than to travel alone.

The lack of in-person socializing wreaked havoc on the single man. He froze in isolation unless he consumed himself with dating apps or resigned himself to digital get-togethers.

Some people enjoyed the sudden changes, inflicting intense anger and dismay on those seeking company. The single man not only had to grin and bear the isolation from his friends, but he also had to listen to their lecturing about staying away from other people. His friends deemed him selfish for seeking human connections. He endured his friends' judgments as they threw their own virtue parties. They would not dare invite this single man.

Anyone would find it bad enough to despair when subjected

to isolation. Worse yet is the knowledge that friends treat the single man, and any man, as an outcast, worthy not even of derision... simply worthy to shun... as we become men with no name, purpose, or future. Our old friends live comfortably in their caves. Little do they realize, they can never take their castles with them to the hereafter, and the castles get stolen from their offspring by the murderous thieves.

Wandering through a Desert of Time

At first you miss the little things... then the big things... then the little things. The cycle continues until you consume yourself with what disappears. You notice what you have, but you wonder when additional activities, places, atmospheres, and people will disappear. You wonder if at some point you will disappear, and then you ask yourself whether you even exist. Others must experience the same desolation. You inhabit a perpetual state of a barren life. Days and nights become lifeless, with all the true fun and vigor sucked out of what remains.

You imagine underground restaurants and musical venues. Images form of word-of-mouth vacation resorts, requiring special tickets for those who pay premiums or get on waiting lists.

The realities of the situation pulverize your imagination and hopes. The realization crystallizes. Pockets exist where people hold closed-off festivities, and even some drunken festivities in the open for all to see. But more often than not, people resign themselves to misery in the physical world and mirage-laden bonds in the digital world. They become comfortable with minimal options. Society finds it simpler to follow orders and judge you for the mere prospect of your disobedience.

Your mind wavers as old connections try to diminish you with a piercing combination of loathing and aversion. You treasure old friends and acquaintances, always noticing the commonalities more than the differences in your relationships. They snub you yet again and avoid communicating. Time to relearn some hard lessons about the bonds you claim to revere. Tenuous connections deteriorate beyond the point of replenishment, and relationships in this new era sour more rapidly than milk curdling in the summer heat.

Adventures to Nowhere

A trapped body can lead to a trapped mind and a trapped spirit.

An isolated body can lead to an isolated mind and an isolated spirit.

Motion is critical. The invisible commotion of desolation frazzles the body, frazzles the mind, and frazzles the soul. There is no rest without motion. There is no motion without rest. Desolation provides neither... only commotion and bewilderment. So my adventurer, where to?

Nature does not adhere to shutdowns. Nature's intransigence leaves open viable options to go outside and walk the ground in front of you. And you can drive to places that become your sanctuary. You seek new areas to explore, yet you look for destinations with the fewest restrictions. Originally, the nearby beach is closed off, but you can drive or walk to it and get some seafood from an open-air shop. And you can still drive right up to the bay.

You focus on what you can do over what you cannot. Ecstatic when the beaches reopen, you see people enjoying life by themselves, with family, with friends. How beautiful it is to see people smiling and enjoying the company of their fellow human beings. Right off the beach, the zone of fear looms over the towns of masked zombies awaiting permission to live again.

Years later, the towns return to normal, but always under the curse of an impending shutdown. The human mind became ingrained with the worries of mandates and store closures.

Even now, as the bars and nightclubs host the eager partygoers, the pure joy from a walk along the streets, the restaurants, and the retail centers disappears. Frequented locations lost their old attractiveness. They close early and do not like you or care about your patronage. Anticipating the restoration of lockdowns, the mind spins on vinyl grooves of madness. It is the same lost vibrancy everywhere the shutdown madness threatens to strike again.

You drive from the Ocean State to the Sunshine State. You find masked zombies everywhere. Despite the lunacy, the drives help. The spirit of exploration motivates you to know the natural world continues apace, and that man-made structures and events can at some point usher in the dawning of a new age of travel. You appreciate what you find right outside your doorstep... even the snake sunbathing in your driveway... the fox running through the woods... the rabbit hopping across the grass.

Hours pass by as you watch the crashing waves just several miles away. You swim in the Atlantic and wash away the worries of a spirit damaged and bewildered.

You spend time on the road. What awe-inspiring pictures of Tennessee music and mansions, a lazy river, and rushing waterfalls. Saw palmettos, palm trees, and Spanish moss adorn the paths of Carolina gators.

Your adventures to nowhere turn into adventures to many places, breaking up the monotony and meeting much welcome strangers. You envision commonalities between you and the locals and travelers alike. How wonderful it is to see faces again. Some smile at you, without their masks... the down-to-earth and the downtrodden.

From tropical islands to cloud-soaked mountains, you rediscover something beyond nature. You rediscover mankind and your role in it. Setting out for the wild blue yonder, you discover people over yonder.

Isolation foreshadows its return in the words and actions of spirit-crushing zombies. When isolation does return, you cannot embark on adventures to nowhere. When isolation returns, you cannot embark on adventures at all until the zombies' masters once again grant ever-so magnanimous permission.

Escape Velocity

The black hole of conformity bears down so strongly that society needs to generate heretofore unused energy to escape the gravity. An individual acting alone is incapable of generating the needed launch capacity himself. He cannot avoid the event horizon's power and rocket past the societal zone of swirling madness. Even if he could somehow escape the black hole as an individual, the devastating gravity of a depraved culture would force him into unrelenting desolation.

The escape velocity at a cultural or societal level must endure the pelting of a demonic asteroid belt. And so escape acceleration has equal importance to escape velocity. Neither the velocity nor acceleration is possible without a critical mass of camaraderie to start the chain reaction.

Camaraderie is the vital but overlooked element. It is not a camaraderie of words or wishes, but a camaraderie of spirited deeds. One must consider the prospects for an emotionally injured man helping his fellow emotionally injured man endure the anguish of imposed and threatened isolations. The time required for everyone to heal their own individual wounds cannot unravel in time for everyone to join as perfect humans. The damaged and imperfect, now more than ever, must act in accordance with a higher calling. It is a calling of purposeful yet lighthearted nonconformity. Individuals must willingly band together in spirit and deed to reclaim civilization from the murderers of all that is just.

Consumption

When the poetry of life resurfaces, some will not be capable of finding rhythms or rhymes. They will never observe or experience beauty in a flowering culture ever again. They will reside in the Petri dish of the past and create unnecessary hells in the future. The multiplying lunacy consumed them. Will it consume us all?

One Trillion Stars of Misery

I hear your misery, my friend, every time I'm in your presence. Your words and your body language annunciate the fear you have in letting me see how much you detest me. Your hatred burns brighter than a trillion stars. Consumed with a quiet rage few can verbalize but many can detect, your face stretches wide, long, and deep.

Frustration overcomes you as you struggle to speak with the respect you pretend to afford me. Such respect from a gentleman who pretends to champion honorable discourse in the midst of a heated battle. Another heated battle dances within you, a scorched man. You are a man charred by bleak visions and memories loaded with regret.

You roll yourself up into a ball of bitterness, seething with past and current thoughts infused in you by your ventriloquists. The ventriloquists control your life and speak words through your mouth as your mind lays dormant. A long sleep ensues, refreshed by neither dreams nor REM cycles. You apply no introspection to a man deluding himself with ideas flimsier than a broken-winged hummingbird.

A grotesque aura captures your grotesque intonations. Yours is a voice understated and ugly, which manifests in the conversations you begin and abandon at the first sign of self-loathing attached to your pseudo intellect. You cannot handle what you construct. You manufacture discussions on the foundations of the same words you demolish without hesitation. Every stilted moment of your expressions, you refuse my architectural support to strengthen your building capacities. How am I to blame for your demolition projects?

You lack the wicked gumption of my acquaintance obsessed with wanton lust. Eyes fueled by the Devil's bile, he does not cringe at the ventriloquists controlling his energy. He knows that to which he falls prey and embraces it. Perhaps his yielding is no better or worse than your tacit acknowledgment of the demons dragging you into a dungeon. They drag you as you ask with a whimper for them to keep you caged.

I witness the other side in a friend who appreciates me and appreciates life. He displays how any thoughtful and caring individual should conduct himself, carefree and unburdened by the demons that often rack him. It is carefree energy that loses to the enraged side of you. You sit in ongoing judgment over the people that compel you to look at your reflection, gorging on agitation more loudly than your veneer of respectability allows you to acknowledge. You devour your own thoughts and dreams with every grimace on your powder-keg frown. Such a slight frown you wear, but one you cannot shelter beneath your phony decorum.

I remain a friend. You offer great hospitality for a limited time... and the expense of suffering your presence. I long for the day when you wake up to your wispy backbone disintegrating from your aura. Until then, you bestow your existence to the ventriloquists battering every part of your vertebrae.

You have my ongoing offer to detach you from your ventriloquists. Allow your bones and mind to recover and shred the trepidation you attempt to spread to me. Just follow the road of a trillion burning stars within. Let them fizzle, or experience the gravity of the hell you carry toward me, your fellow man. The choice is yours. In the meantime, you can find me watching the magic of solar winds and lunar seas. I enmesh myself in these God-given sights and sounds to behold, unrelated to your one trillion stars of misery.

Societal Assassins

Death hovers over us, with the promise of murder.

We already witness the slow-motion murder of civilization. It is a murder so horrific, stemming from the act of destruction itself... and from the methods of annihilation.

The story unfolds in the here and now. We experience our story through our mind's absorption of unfolding events. From our mind, we gaze across the constellation of the present.

Societal assassins carve up every piece of civilization they can, slicing at the vessels and dissecting the nerve center and still beating heart. We know we could be next. Our hometown assassins close in on us and what's left of our family.

Our city lies at the center of doom. In this city, time and space crumble. Scavengers roam freely throughout the widening zone of horror. Civilization gasps for oxygen, as do we, every night in our sleep, and every day throughout this lurid freak show.

Every moment passes with agony. The milliseconds bring with them excruciating knowledge that society tumbles under a great wave of hell. The clock ticks inch forward. Time decelerates the tumbling, but society drowns in the rip currents.

We attempt to pivot at an inflection point, but the second-hand strikes midnight. We watch and wait as our community suffers an indelible and mortal wound. Losing all hope and striving, we recognize we have no power to reverse the trauma to our city, society, or civilization.

Time offers us no solace or saving grace. We experience a warped flow of time that traps us in moments we can never escape.... Or so we think... Time, whether moving slowly or rapidly, cannot change the destiny of a civilization already missing much of its life force.

We do not yet know if a civilization murdered causes our own individual losses of life. We do know we can draw on the power of time to move forward along life's path and support others on their own journeys.

At some point, society finds enough space to engage in a critical mass of frivolous pursuits. This point in time oscillates with the torrents running through the age of wreckage. Despite great builders and inventors, the civilization housing this society moves into recorded and unrecorded history. Now society has too much time to watch itself on the inevitable road to losing its breath forever, pulling civilization into the sharpened blades of the societal assassins. Time merges into space as they journey together into civilizational death.

We have a front-row seat to watch civilization die at the hands of societal assassins. Our city marks the starting point for where the murder occurs. We continue our expedition to new realms to find respite from the unquenchable rage ravaging the land. All the best people and creations fall prey to the assassins. Our eyes suffer the sights of manmade marvels dismantled, and our ears endure the resonance of sonatas silenced.

Our city does not differ from other cities of yesteryear and tomorrow. We had a thriving metropolis, offering recreational land, awe-inspiring architecture, and artistry worthy of the buildings showcasing them. If we leave the city, we have no place to go to avoid the knives of the societal assassins. We move around anyhow, thinking time can provide the added space within which we might witness the reversal of all that sullied our landscape.

Fluctuations between confidence and despair continue within our spirits. We ingest the full force of civilization's death. Alchemy replaces science. Emotionalism replaces wisdom. Whimsical passions replace dedication. A never-ending void replaces purpose. Wicked sacrifice replaces meaningful sacrifice. These elements affect the society in which we live, the minds from which we perceive, and the souls with which we understand. We see the shades and shadows of a civilization in irreversible decline.

Men carry on traversing a deadly terrain of tectonic cultural transformations. We bid farewell to our once great civilization, now mortally wounded in the death grip of societal assassins.

SNAPSHOTS (FLASH FICTION I)

A ftershock

Charlotte developed deep sorrow, even though she always lived life as a naturally happy soul. The shutdowns ended a while back, but the damage to her sense of security would not relent, despite her mother's caring presence.

Remnants of the health measures continued to haunt Charlotte. She could not shake her unease about the dogma she noticed in those meant to provide care. Her mother tried to console her to no avail.

What did Charlotte see on the floor that sent her into a tailspin? The markings simply noted to stay six feet apart.

Why should something as simple as physical distancing in a medical office be so disturbing? It could not be the physical distancing alone. The friendly faces of the medical staff disappeared.

Masks erased not only faces but warmth as well. Protocol turned into a covenant between science and Satan.

Charlotte understood the evil of the virus protection rules more than most people. She had receptors of mental and emotional sorrow that kept her isolated from those who could not comprehend her pain. Her mother held her tightly, yet no parent's love could fight back the hell unleashed by the shutdown gods.

This is but one story of an aftershock consuming the mentally and emotionally disabled.

Charlotte's time on Earth became forever damaged. She was one of many whom jackals turned into a casualty of a civilizational earthquake.

Hope Shined through a Woman's Beautiful Face

As matters turned south with Denise, Eric suffered a gut-wrenching defeat in his soul. He could not fully experience the festive atmosphere around him. That was Denise's unconscious goal. Her demons had enveloped her and were too powerful for Eric to handle.

Just when Eric felt fully deflated, he walked by a woman sitting alone and felt her subtle energy. He never got her name, but she smiled at him, and he smiled back. The woman's smile restored hope to Eric that not all gorgeous countenances deceive their recipients.

A certain kindness carries no expectations or pre-packaged lies. Eric discovered this sort of kindness at a low point, and it propelled him to see that a lot of decency finds its way into life simply by looking for it. In this case, he found it in spades with a woman's smile. He escaped the power of Denise's demons and continued his quest for a bright present and a bright future.

Guilt

Was it too much to ask for me to be Jeffrey's friend? We were kids, but how could I not still feel guilt for looking down on him those many years ago.

Though rare for me to join a chorus mocking Jeffrey, at times I sang in the chorus. On certain days I watched his dad pick him up from school. The happiness and pride on his father's face was too much for me to bear. In spirit and deed, I put down a man's treasured son.

Decades later, my guilt burns brightly.

Out of Reach

Jennifer sought the life of a fairy tale. One in which the prince would become a serf in order to prop her up as a leading noble in his stead. At the same time she wished paradoxically for a utopian prince to fit every vision of what she thought a prince should be.

The morose princess could not be happy whether she achieved a rich man, a poor man, an everyman, a strange man, an enlightened man, or any man whatsoever. Jennifer sought the darkness and a man that would join her in a dungeon of despair. Steven could not oblige this invitation to the dungeon, and so Jennifer traipsed ceaselessly along her maze until she could imprison a man and herself until their deaths. She wondered every hour why she felt so alone. The princess could not perceive that her self-constructed maze shielded her from the very senses she needed to detect how willingly she chose a perpetual inferno on Earth.

Jennifer's maze led to the dungeon of despair as she passed the threshold of ever escaping. Steven never knew how fortunate he was to slip away from Jennifer's grasp... but slip away he did from the grasping fires of never-ending perdition.

At Long Last

Doug and Celeste formed a special bond... a bond that would diminish in a slow motion they could neither hasten nor reverse. A connection between two materialistic souls having no sense of true loyalty, kinship, or love. Each of them, impressed by the images they had of themselves in their minds and mirrors.

The couple climbed the social ladders with reckless abandon.

They received compliments that brought their heads above the clouds and into the far reaches of space. Such emotion they had for each other and their lives together. Doug and Celeste soared... alone and together they soared. Restaurants, parties, vacations, and benefits. They soared on the energy of their own wings, and they achieved an excitement flying closer to the sun than any tragic figure from the ancient world.

Doug and Celeste sputtered without a propeller or sufficient gasoline to sustain their lifelong pursuits. The couple did not crash and burn. Husband and wife descended slowly and entered an inexorable wormhole on the lowest level of the troposphere.

Hold the Elevator

Going up or down? Eddie wanted a ride up to the highest floor with Stephanie.

Eddie pressed the button to go to the top, but before they reached it, the elevator reversed course and descended... and kept descending.

Just as Eddie thought they reached the bottom floor, they descended until it stopped long enough for him to depart the opening doors. Ronnie told Eddie to hold the elevator. But Eddie rushed out.

Stephanie pressed the button to reopen the closing doors, and Ronnie spent time with her all the way down to the basement.

Ronnie couldn't get out... the elevator was stuck at the bottom and he couldn't pry open the doors.

Eddie walked out of the building, a little perplexed, but a free man.

Sad Avatars

Alive or dead? Kurt became an old video game character controlled by multiple players' joysticks. He knew he was born into the real world, breathing, eating, and finding shelter.

Regrettably, Kurt's time as a virtual reality cartoon increased with the passing years. He stopped breathing after spending decades as both man and character. No longer a sentient physical being, he lived on through his images, social media caricature, and virtual activities. Kurt's family provided no in-person memorial service for his passing. His loved ones offered praise and sorrow on the newest platforms... a memorial service for descendants to experience anytime and anywhere.

Kurt's family and friends bragged about his life, death, actions, and memory at their disposal. He would live and die forever in the seventh circle of avatar hell.

Corned Beef Sandwich

Jack orders the corned beef and almost pays the ultimate price...

A real person, Jack epitomizes a living ghost, often ignored and rarely remembered.

He looks around the pub and the sandwich arrives.

He notices from the first couple of bites that the corned beef has a lot of fat.

On the third bite, the food lodges in his windpipe.

He gasps for a clear breath as nobody around sees him losing air.

In a flash, Jack notices an eternity of people talking and laughing.

Couples...

Friends...

Pub staff...

All oblivious to Jack.

Not all of the food in the sandwich created the obstruction.

Only the corned beef failed to move down the esophagus.

In a moment of quick thinking combined with instinct...

A force guides Jack's right hand to reach in his mouth and pull out the corned beef.

He pulls it from the top, and the corn beef slides out along with the fat.

Windpipe clear...

Esophagus clear...

A little disoriented, Jack regains his bearings.

He once again looks around... nobody the wiser that he almost lost his life.

He leaves the rest of the food on his plate, has some water, and pays the bill.

The drink tastes more refreshing than any glass of water in recent memory.

Jack left the restaurant as he entered it... a living ghost.

Spaceship

The old shuttle flies through disaster. Damaged and disoriented from the asteroid belt, a valiant spacecraft on course for Jupiter. Countless disasters in the shuttle's life. The ship's exterior, littered with dents and permanent blemishes.

This time, the shuttle contends with space rocks instead of the usual space debris. Any sturdy ship can weather tiny fragments... no matter how fast the tiny fragments or sturdy the ship.

The old spacecraft finds itself the unwitting target of unconscious asteroids. A random bullseye on the spacefaring ship of doom. Fate compels the shuttle to veer off its mission.

The shuttle cannot reach Jupiter intact. No matter how sturdy... no matter how determined. One large rock clipping would kill the spacecraft.

Asteroids rain down as the ship veers back toward Mars. The shuttle zigzags and dodges all the space boulders pinpointing the capsule. The ship failed to reach the Red Planet... but it lives! Sturdy as can be, the old shuttle would never approach the atmosphere of the Jovian Promised Land.

My Dog

Today lasted more than one billion millennia. What could go wrong did go wrong. No preconceived notions or negative thoughts on what would happen. Things just didn't turn out well. A litany of troubles hounded me from one hour to the next, with no quarter until getting home.

It was not my home that helped me. It was my dog. Noticing my sadness, he greeted me with the concern that only a dog could show. He offered no degrading critiques on my state of mind. He would not chastise me for suffering defeats. He did not ignore me or cast me away into a pit of has-beens.

My dog stayed by my side. On a day when my girlfriend left me. On a day when my boss scolded me. On a day when I had no one to talk to. I had but one friend, and I went to sleep smiling at the train wreck of a day, knowing things weren't so bad after all.

Vicious

An hour after midnight. One man stands apart during the New Year's celebration. His eyes filled with the bitterness he longs to inflict on others. A hatred so palpable that a visible energy field coalesces to separate him from the wasted partygoers. Though a human being, he moves about the nightclub with the bearing of an injured leopard.

He carries a look far beyond that of desired vengeance or wanton brawling. He is a man in the throes of death. A matter of time before he tempts another human wildcat to shred him. A destiny six feet under before halfway to 60. This is what he desires, and on the way to his box underground, he hopes to murder another wildcat and enjoy doing it.

A man born to destroy. No love circulating his mind or body. He seeks an end to himself and anybody blurring his field of vision. The wasted partygoers continue their night of drinks and dancing. The injured leopard surveys the field to taunt someone into a dance of smashing fists. Targets step away as he pushes, bumps, and threatens. Nobody takes the bait on this night.

Just one year later, a human tiger seals his fate.

Ferris Wheel

I walk the town fair on a warm November afternoon. Not knowing why I'm here, aside from the distraction the fair grants me from a society in peril. Around the town I stroll, trying to let go the sense of impending privation. Privation for all but an exclusive cadre of self-selected chosen ones and their technocrats. I don't see any rides, but I remember the Ferris wheel from last year.

Moving toward the heart of the festivities. Always a fine show to watch a juggler hurl fire sticks in the air without a burn or stumble. It's 1:00 PM, and the inebriated town fair attendees launch themselves into thunderous cackles of joy at the juggler. The rallying cry bellows out, "another round before lunch!" Families keep their distance from the already rowdy. Pumpkin pies and art displays attract the briefest of visitors to the community's yearly gathering of funnel cakes and circuses. An aroma of cotton candy merges with the stench of cheap beer. The rides have to be somewhere around here.

Not the best daytime venture... but a welcome break from forthcoming darkness. Ready to leave the fair as the clouds gather and a cool wind gains power. What a happily depressed town this has become. Strange, there are no rides at the fair this year. Not even a Ferris wheel.

Citizen's Escapade

Off I go to make my views count for something vital to my community and humanity. An important day, with everything at stake. Time for me to cast my lot with the views that matter most. Such division and hatred gripping all of us. Difficult for me to express the gratefulness I have for being able to side with the righteous.

This journey to make my views heard does not come easily. I leave work early despite the maddening deadlines I must meet behind my cubicle day in and day out. Proud I am, to have a boss so willing to let me go early and exercise a right I never want to take for granted. An inalienable right afforded to me by birth and citizenship. On this special day, my boss does not need to ask why I am leaving as early as I am. And of course, I do not have to actually say why. I submit my work for the day and go to fulfill my civic responsibility as I pass the smiling and understanding faces of my peers.

Heavy rain greets me at the door! I pause for a moment and consider going back inside. But I cannot stop now. So much hangs in the balance that I would dwell in embarrassment for not living up to my obligation. I must run across the parking lot to my vehicle. My run quickly slows to a walk. Still full from lunch. Yet as I start the ignition, I feel the pride that generations feel in doing their part to gain what satisfaction they can in a free society.

Here I am. Stepping out of my vehicle, I do not notice that I am right next to the grass on the driver's side. I step out and take a giant step into the mud. My shoes and pant cuffs, dirty and soaked, I move toward the building with a big sign outside to let me know I am in the right place. Joy. Contentment. A hunger to fulfill my obligation. Lucky for me, I show up before the crowds. And here it is...

My favorite pizza joint! I have a commitment to consume delicious slices with meatballs and pepperoni. I can never break that commitment, no matter the cost. Some people hate it here and swear their allegiance to the unsalvageable hot dog cart down the street. I know where I stand and hot dogs pose a risk to all of society. I cannot let my favorite pizza joint perish in the sands of time and stand idly by as a hot dog cart tries to take over the community.

We must all meet our responsibility to the best establishment in town. I carried out my commitment with purpose and sacrifice. I hope that as many people as possible make their voices heard... or at least exercise rights to consume pizza and ostracize hot dogs! Are those rights or privileges? I can never remember. All I know is I could use some cookies from the bakery, but I cannot figure out if that would harm democracy.

Gut Punch at the Roller Rink

Ronnie gets pushed around. That's the story of his life, for as far back as he can remember, and he's eight years old. Eight years old and already sensing he's predestined to years of being mocked and bullied. Predestined if he doesn't change course.

He just doesn't know how to shake off the aggressors or stand up for himself. He's determined to find out how.

The roller rink draws in lots of people every weekend. On this particular Saturday, Ronnie goes there with several friends, just like he does every Saturday. Skating through the arcade area, an older kid named Jake punches Ronnie in the stomach. It's the first time Rodney gets punched, and he can't catch his breath. Gasping for air, his breathing slowly returns to normal. Now he knows what it's like to get the wind knocked out of him. Jake's friends cannot leave the situation alone. They taunt Ronnie and his friends on the skating rink, but Ronnie resolves he will not leave the floor. He knows that if he backs down now, he cannot break the pattern. As he thinks about how to break the cycle, one of Jake's friends launches toward Ronnie to push him over onto the hardwood rink. Ronnie sidesteps out of the way at the last second... not on purpose. Ronnie just moves with the rhythm of the 80's music. He glides forward as Jake's friend crashes into the wall and falls to the ground, a lot more embarrassed than hurt.

Ronnie emerges as a wiser kid than before the gut punch. Jake puts the taunting to an end with no further patience for what he knows is his own role in starting the situation. He feels like he is the one out of breath and gasping for air. He feels the gut punch of going after someone who poses no threat and starts no problems. Jake apologizes to Ronnie, and both their stomachs return to normal. Ronnie takes a deep breath. For years in the future, he glides on and off the roller rink to avoid disaster. He owes it all to a watchful eye over him on a victorious Saturday in the 1980s.

Trial by Judge

A man's life hangs in the balance...

Jason agrees to stand trial. He knows that with a guilty verdict, everything would end. He cannot plea bargain either. Guilty or not guilty? Time will tell, and so will the judge.

No jury for these proceedings. Jason sees the case as a clear-cut opportunity to defend himself, establishing irrefutable innocence, much less obvious doubt. He has dealt with the judge before. This judge can be sensible and merciful. Yet she can be illogical and harsh.

Jason realizes he stands trial as a repeat offender in the eyes of the court. The court is the judge, and the judge is the court. She holds sway over Jason's guilt or innocence, regardless of the truth.

Not much can happen during the proceedings, other than for Jason to answer questions directly from the judge. No witnesses reveal themselves in the trial. Nobody cross-examines Jason, and he has nobody to cross-examine.

The judge deliberates in a matter of minutes. The verdict is guilty on all counts!

Jason wonders if hiring representation could help him in the sentencing trial. But the judge decides against a sentencing trial and she makes up her mind on the spot.

Jason wonders if representation could help him with an appeal. The odds disfavor an appeal, but he wants to go for it.

The appeal crumbles upon suggestion. Denied with fervor. Jason sits with his hands covering his face. Dejected and out of options, he accepts the guilty verdict and sentencing.

Guilty of leaving clothes on the floor.

Guilty of leaving used dishes on the counter.

Guilty of never buying flowers.

Guilty of not caring enough about his wife.

Jason's wife, the judge, stands in the living room and doles out the sentencing... a nighttime of insults and a lifetime of grudges. Somehow, Jason considers himself fortunate. He considers himself lucky for never receiving the worst charge possible... the charge of sleeping with his wife's best friend. For that he is guilty, yet he cannot be convicted for that which he is not charged.

Now and forever, Jason must endure a marriage filled with grudges. His household and symbolic misdeeds live in wedded infamy. He could turn himself in for adultery. He does not. For all his crimes and convictions, Jason understands that such an admission would be his last time in front of the judge. At least he can enjoy house arrest and watch television if he keeps his mouth shut.

Sea Monster

A terrifying creature springs into being.

Lava cools across the ocean floor and forms a rigid layer the Crintaggle calls home.

The Crintaggle, a giant triple-horned dragon, with the seismic roar of a super tiger and the tornado-force jaws of a mega gator.

The dragon ascends thousands of feet to the surface, inflicting murder on any animal caught on its warpath.

Dolphins reach full speed to escape the monster.

Humpback whales sing urgent harmonies to warn their brethren.

The Crintaggle launches over the surface, crashing back down under water a minute later and catapulting fish and mammals through the nighttime sky.

His dive sends a tidal wave that submerges buildings and beach towns into extinction.

Not Meant to Be

Samantha lassos Jeff's attention at the wedding reception. Jeff introduces himself to her, and she to him. They hit it off immediately. An instant attraction upon first glance. The mutual allure nearly becomes too much for either one to bear. When the conversation begins, Jeff envisions Samantha as his future wife. Two years from his divorce, this becomes the first time since the marital collapse that he can envision marital happiness.

To Jeff and Samantha, the wedding guests disappear from the reception. The bride and groom disappear. The whispers and gasps of the bride's family disappear. All that exists is the conversation between a man and woman, both with little regard for the bride and groom that invited them out of habit. In a magical time and place, Jeff and Samantha found each other and arranged an exclusive party for two.

Conversation reaches its height... just before the magic disappears and the onlookers reappear. Jeff suddenly hears the wedding guest murmuring and senses their looks. He recognizes the father of the bride scoffing as Samantha tells Jeff her husband could not make it to the wedding. Samantha feels every string on her heartstrings. She utters the word "husband" with a gelatinous mix of shame, regret, relief, and warning. Jeff slinks back to reality, ready to put his divorce and his imaginary relationship with Samantha behind him.

Promised Journey

Fred found himself on flat land, surrounded by towering mountains, and his ancestors with him. Fred misses directions from a group nearby for what measures he should take to climb to towering heights. He sees an old acquaintance walk by among the other groups of visitors. Fred shakes his old acquaintance's

hand and remembers the dreams of his childhood. It is sum-
mertime, and not a trace of snow remains in the mountains.

The day is mostly clear, with only passing clouds floating across
the peaks. Fred has the slight sense of enemies lurking some-
where nearby, but he has to make the climb. He does not know
which route to follow. His ancestors walk along a flat path. They
have no more mountains to climb on Earth. Fred faces the truth
that he must follow a path up a mountain top. He must hike
alone to discover what awaits him on the way. He must hike
alone to discover what awaits him in the valley. Fred calls to his
ancestors as they walk into the distance, knowing a land he must
journey toward awaits him. They hear him, but something tells
him they are not permitted to respond. Their ears perk up as
they turn their heads halfway.

Fred does not know if he will reach the promised land of his
existence. He does know he must take the promised journey. He
prays the spirits of his ancestors and all his loved ones will help
guide him along the way.

Very Fast

Born. Blink. 80 years.

Shutdown

Friends. Shutdowns. Enemies.

Beyond the Reach of Pharaoh

I cannot stand up to Pharaoh. Nobody can. It is an impossible task for me to undertake alone or with all the people on Earth. I need help that takes me beyond the long arm of Pharaoh. God will help me overcome all the dark power of my enslaver.

Pharaoh sends his legions to find me. They track me across the sands and discover nothing but the dry winds beating their faces. Dry winds leading them through a web of calamity. One legion after another falls prey to desert storms and disappears from the living realm. The living realm over which their master, Pharaoh, has no dominion, and whose fleeting time approaches the end.

Destroying the fabric of many peoples, Pharaoh shudders. He cannot imprison me. The land and seas consume his legions. I homestead in the oasis of my God and witness the crumbling of a ghastly authoritarian. I wonder who or what will rise in his place. God will provide all the answers I need, at the right moments and places, for me or anyone else invited to homestead on His oasis.

Luck

Smiling and exuberant, she exudes dignity, an effortless inductor of cheerful currents.

The night grows older and colder as she walks away. I never did get her name. Remnants of an opportunity not seized.

St. Patrick's Day came and went. The electric woman would prevail as an illusion, as would, in my case, the luck of the Irish.

Knights in Rusted Armor

Chivalry arrives, served with a twist of sorcery. Lauren knows her suitors have no desire to win her as a spouse. The men courting her pursue a legacy of destroying as many damsels as possible. Lauren pours out her drinks of chivalry, knowing she will never drink the mashed up pill of sorcery. The knights in rusted armor move onto their next desired trophies. Lauren waits patiently for the knight who refuses to partake in casting the spells or mixing the solutions of an evil wizard.

LENSES (FLASH FICTION II)

Patrick's Virtual Spacesuit

Patrick Jones lives in fear of illness. He worries day and night about what viruses and bacteria plan to burst through the shadows to afflict him. Patrick shudders at the thought of fungus or protozoa destroying his life. He lives life dreading an autoimmune illness or the death of an organ. Wearing a spacesuit would calm him for an instant, but in his mind, the suit would be too thin or too easily permeated.

Sickness everywhere! Patrick lives alone. He imagines infectious disease in everyone and keeps his distance. Coughing, sneezing, chills. Germs threaten to spread into his bloodstream at every moment. Patrick can think of nothing to protect his nasal passages, mouth, or eyelids from contaminants in the air. He confines himself to an exclusive existence in virtual reality, minimizing the chance of waning health spread by sloppy breathers. No death can visit Patrick anytime soon. He outflanks the microorganisms and the decline of his body.

Living in solitude, Patrick's mind begins to rot. He creates a sterile atmosphere, not understanding the self-contained life is not so sterile after all. No matter how sanitary an atmosphere, Patrick cannot wash away the specters that haunt him. His mind deforms in his state of fraudulent sterilization. He sees the fatal flaw in a plan to protect his body at the expense of his spirit, curiosity, and desire to live.

When Patrick finally bears all the isolated madness he can handle, he steps back into the world. Wanting to form a family and surround himself with people he could see all the time, he strips off his costume. He throws out his virtual space suit and breathes the imperfect air once again. Patrick regains the happiness he lost, rediscovering events, activities, and work. He gets married and begins a family. Elated at being outside, he watches his mind, experiencing the unbridled joy of a normal human being. Patrick finds happiness in life amidst the occasional sickness that he grows to accept. Peace of mind overtakes him, and impurities in people and atmospheres no longer control him.

As a pandemic rages, Patrick dusts off his virtual spacesuit and dons it without hesitation. The specters return as he reconvenes his old suspicions. He looks at his wife in a fear that belies old worries and paralyzes life. Patrick feels justified, yet always unsafe from illness in the age of the pandemic. Try as he might to stay healthy, the rampant virus overtakes him and trashes his lungs.

A dying Patrick longs to see his wife. Suddenly he remembers in his hospital bed that she now wears her own virtual spacesuit, in a different city, and cannot allow him to infect her body. Patrick dies, a lonely astronaut, crashing and burning within a hospital room. Every region of his mind becomes re-infected with fear. Through their permeable virtual spacesuits, Patrick's wife's mind remains infused with the infectious disease of permanent horror.

Platinum City

Justin lived in a remote hamlet nestled in the mountains. He dreamed of moving to Platinum City, but he had neither the resources nor the job prospects to bring him there. He walked about his hamlet, angry that he could not leave. The townspeople greeted him with good cheer despite the insults he hurled at them.

One man, Xander, faced Justin's continuous mocking. Xander had walked with a limp since childhood. Born with a physical condition that prevented his ability to run, he lived as a kindhearted boy who grew up to be a kindhearted adult. He paid no mind to Justin's insults, instead wishing for Justin to find his way to Platinum City to find joy.

On the evening of an unexpected snowfall, Justin became especially disturbed by his own demons. He took out these demons on Xander in the hamlet's cobblestone square.

"Where are you off to this evening?" said Justin. "A little difficult to run on an evening such as this... so icy, and so easy to slip and fall. Then again, is it not always difficult for you to run?"

"For years you insult me," said Xander. "My body struggles to move, and somehow you take offense at this. Have I done something to harm you? All I wish for you are great things. Why must you show me such bitterness?"

"It's all in good fun," said Justin, disturbed by Xander's question. "You can't walk and it looks funny. It's not as though I want you to die! I make fun of everyone. That's how I survive in this terrible town. The air in this alpine village is as thin as the skin of its inhabitants. None of you have any sense of humor, and you all deserve my mockery. Some of you are even worthy of my scorn. You are fortunate not to be one of them. You are fortunate not to be one of those worthy of my enthusiastic ridicule."

"I find great fortune in being alive," said Xander. "It is a blessing to have all my senses and be able to walk, no matter how slowly or painfully. There is great fortune in helping the shopkeepers and tradesmen, my family and my fellow townspeople. I see tremendous misfortune in the bitterness that wears away at the lining of your heart. Will nobody else talk to you besides me?"

"Like I said, you are fortunate to be one of those not receiving the full intensity of my jokes," said Justin.

"Justin, let me know when you become free of the curse that controls you," said Xander, with reverence for a long-lost friend. "This self-inflicted curse is one with which you were not born, and which you did not suffer through tragedy. I wish an end to the spell that manipulates you. I pray you find the happiness in your heart that ran away in your childhood."

Xander continued walking across the square as Justin stood dumbfounded. Justin wondered, "Did Xander just reverse a spell on me? He gave me no magic potion. I just heard the words of a man I despise, and no longer do I despise him. No longer do I despise anyone. This is a glorious day!"

Justin resolved to make amends with everyone in the hamlet. He resolved to thank Xander later that day, as Xander lived only a few cottages away on their snow-blanketed road. Justin returned home as night descended. He received a written message left on a windowsill.

"We received your correspondence, and we need you working as a merchant with us in Platinum City. Await our follow-on message as we arrange transportation for you and a cottage for your new home. Platinum City Food Merchants."

An elated Justin went to Xander's cottage to thank him, but Xander was not home.

Blizzard conditions developed and worsened through the evening.

In the morning, the sun shone brightly, and the storm ended. A new storm moved in for Justin as he left his cottage to attempt once again to see Xander.

On Justin's short walk on the icy road, he slipped and fell. The fall was life-altering, and he broke his back and could not walk. Residents of the hamlet saw Justin lying on the frozen surface in agony, and they helped him that day the same way they would help anyone on any day.

Xander would visit Justin's cottage every day, blizzard or shine, autumn through spring. Justin would never walk again. He would never make his way to Platinum City.

Just Keep Living, Part I

Police pronounce Kevin's parents dead at the scene. Eleven-year-old Kevin walks away without a scratch, surviving his family's tumbling vehicle. A drunk driver blindsided them, and neighbors witness the incident and aftermath in shock. Kevin watches the police walk off the handcuffed drunk driver to jail. Police hold the killer upright as he stumbles and looks over without remorse at a traumatized Kevin. The child must confront the realization that his loving parents are gone. With no other close family nearby, Kevin's grandfather, Eddie, flies in from the Grand Tetons to Newark, New Jersey.

At the end of a terrifying day, Eddie picks up Kevin from a distant cousin's house. They go to the empty house in Demarest, New Jersey. Yesterday, Kevin's parents took him apple picking.

Today, Kevin's parents are gone forever. Tomorrow, Kevin will feel a sense of unrelenting hopelessness.

"Kevin, the last thing I wanna do is take you from the home you've known your whole life," says Eddie. "Next week, I'm taking you with me to Wyoming for a while. Grandma and I are going to take care of you."

Kevin looks at his grandfather, puzzled and upset. "Grandpa, I just want Mom and Dad back."

"So do I, Kevin. So do I." Eddie, not a man given to crying, feels a great irritation in his eyes. He does not yield to the threatened onslaught of tears, and his sunglasses conceal any hint of what he suppresses.

Kevin hugs his grandfather. "Can I visit New Jersey again?"

"Of course you can," says Eddie with a smile. "Grandma and I will go with you."

For an instant, Kevin has a sense hope restored.

Eddie keeps his promise. He flies back to New Jersey several times with Kevin over the next seven years. Two of the four times are with Kevin's grandmother, who dies shortly after Kevin enters his sophomore year in high school.

Just shy of seven years after the crash, Eddie flies into Newark with Kevin for a week before college begins. Kevin goes to school back east, and he and his grandfather fly back-and-forth over holidays and summers for many years to follow. On the day

Eddie drops Kevin off at college, he helps him get settled into the dormitory. They talk outside before Eddie heads to Newark Airport.

"I can't tell you how happy I am about what you've done," says Eddie. "Your parents and grandma would be extremely proud."

Kevin drops his head. "Grandma never saw me get off drugs."

"Hey, pick your head up. You've been sober two years now. She would be very proud of you."

"Grandpa, I was so mean to her. I was so mean to you and everyone else. I was such a dirt bag. I wish-"

"Just stop right there. We know you're not a saint, but what your grandma and I knew is that you had a genuine kindness that will travel with you everywhere you go. You just have to trust it. I know you get tempted to let out your devil. You've got to let that part of you die. Life will be so much better for you and everyone around you when you do. Besides, you don't want me flying in and visiting you every weekend and embarrassing you in front of all your friends."

"Grandpa! You always make me laugh!" He hugs his grandfather closely and counts the days until he sees him again.

Kevin loves his grandfather with all his heart. Twenty-nine years after the drunk driver kills Eddie's son and daughter-in-law, it is Eddie who stands on the edge of death. A 40-year-old Kevin feels immobilized with fear, wanting to hold on to his grandfather no matter the cost.

Welcome to Eddie's home in the mountains of Wyoming, one of the last bastions of rural America to survive. Kevin visits from New York City to pay his respects at his grandfather's modest ranch home on a small lake. The lake house inundates Kevin with childhood memories of his now deceased parents. For a long time, after much tragedy and the passing of loved ones, he tried to put aside the thought of what it means to move onto the hereafter. With his grandfather's impending passing, the afterlife moves into Kevin's vision once again. He aims to learn any last lesson he can from his grandfather. Eddie takes on the challenge of leaving a lasting gift to Kevin, his only grandson. He greets Kevin at the door.

"Hi grandpa," says Kevin, smiling from ear to ear, upon seeing the man he admires most.

The two men embrace, and Eddie looks over his grandson with a happiness reserved for the best moments in life.

"For an old man, you move around really well," says Kevin. "I can hardly believe you're dying."

"Kevin, I know you don't believe it," says Eddie. "I know you won't believe this either, but you have a lot of great things left in life. What brings my grandson so far from home? What's got you so deflated?"

"I wanted to see you before you died, Grandpa. I wanted to spend time with the only person who really cares about me, and the only family I have left."

"You have nothing to be afraid of. All the old ghosts that haunted you long ago died off. Terrible as it is, you had to grow up without parents, and you dealt with it as well as any child could. The drunk driver robbed you. That you survived was a miracle. Eleven years old is far too young an age to lose parents, but remember that the drunk driver robbed me of my son and your mom, who was a daughter. You lost two parents, while I lost two children."

"Grandpa, I've been thinking about them a lot lately. More than usual, I've been thinking about our trips to see you. I wonder if—"

"Hold on a moment. I'm not as frail as you thought I'd be."

"Stop trying to make me laugh. You know you don't look frail at all."

"You are laughing, aren't you?"

"Yes, Grandpa, as always."

"Good! Now that we've greeted each other, why don't you tell me why you're really here?"

Just Keep Living, Part II

Eddie knows Kevin is here in Wyoming to see him before he dies, but he sees the nerves and the hint of panic swirling around his grandson.

Kevin cannot help but feel exposed by his grandpa's question, "why don't you tell me why you're really here? His granddad knows all his tricks. Kevin does not want to admit what follows him from New York City to the pastoral setting of an endangered American landscape.

The old pristine lakes and forests hold memories outside the harsh realities of Kevin's city life. He cannot escape, no matter how far he travels. He feels the weight of this, combined with the stark realization that his grandfather's days continue dwindling.

"Everywhere is unrecognizable," says Kevin. "I don't understand where I am. People look at me with frowns and scowls. I see no light in their eyes. I can still see the indifference of the drunk driver taking my parents' life. It's as though he multiplied to become everyone in the city. That's not the New York City I remember or the life I remember. Everything is different, and everyone is cold."

"You traveled a couple thousand miles to tell me people are cold. What are you hiding from me?"

"I'm saying that without you, I don't have anyone left."

"Are you sure about that? That sounds a little depressing."

Kevin laughs. "Grandpa, you're being funny again."

"Excellent! I just want to see you laugh. It's one of the few things I really care about seeing in my last moments."

"Whaddaya mean your last moments? You might be dying, but you're not dying tonight."

"Kevin, I'll be gone before you know it. Things move quickly. Time moves quickly. You just need to know that you have a lot more than you think. You'll always have people who care about you. Your parents are gone, and so is your grandmother. Your extended family is so troubled and consumed by hatreds, it's difficult to call them family. But your parents. Your grandmother. You have people who passed on, but that doesn't mean that their love for you died with them. That love continues even after you die. The same will be true of me. My love for you continues, and nothing erases that. Not my death. Not your death. Nothing."

"That means a lot to me, Grandpa. I have little in the way of friends, and I have no family of my own."

"There's time yet for that. Even if you were never to have a family of your own, you've meant something to people's lives. You've provided them with valuable friendship and they've reciprocated. You may not have a lot of friends, but some of us, like me, don't have friends at all. I know you've lost many people in different ways. There's nothing you can do about that. Whether you've lost them because of death or abandonment, you're not by yourself. You're still cared for, and me and your grandmother and your parents aside, you've got a lot going for you in the compassion you show other people. That might not be obvious to you, but there isn't much that's more important than being helpful."

"We both know I've been very ungrateful to you and to old

friends. I don't know why I—."

"You haven't been ungrateful to me," says Eddie. "If you were, then you wouldn't be visiting me in my final chapter of life."

"I'm frightened, Grandpa. I know a man isn't supposed to be frightened. A man isn't supposed to show it or feel it or anything like that. But I can't lie to myself. I'm frightened, and that makes me revisit the car wreck. It's been so many years, but I haven't been this frightened since the car wreck."

"Forget about what you should or shouldn't feel. Why are you here… other than to pay respects to your dying grandfather?"

"I don't know. Maybe I'm looking for answers."

"Believe me, I know you're looking for answers, but what answers are you looking for?"

"Well, I don't know what to do next, and I feel like a child. I'm drifting off from who I am and what I'm supposed to do."

"Kevin, I can't tell you what to do, but I can tell you it's the moves you make that count. Let go of how you're supposed to feel, or whether you're a real man. You have another friend, but he's a friend you've often seen as an enemy. He's your God-given spirit, and he's the greatest gift you have. When you follow him, you'll begin seeing all the wondrous things around you that you used to see. You'll see these things whether you're in the concrete jungle or the snowcapped peaks overlooking the lakes and valleys. Stop telling yourself what you're supposed to do. Start letting your spirit guide the way to who you are, and then leave me alone so I can die in peace."

"You'll always make me laugh, Grandpa. When you're gone, you'll still make me laugh."

"That's right, and I'll live on after I'm gone. When it's your turn to die, you'll live on, too. You've got a while before you go, so keep living. Just keep on living. I'll be with you for all time, my dearest grandson. God as my witness, my love for you will survive the loss of my body. Just keep living. If you do, that will be the best gift an old man can give his grandson. Take the gift of knowing you have lots of life in you to better yourself and things around you when you can. Keep me in mind every now and again, would ya?"

"Grandpa, I miss you already, but I have a gift for you as well. In life and in the hereafter, God willing, I will be with you as much as you are with me."

"You're giving me a better gift than I could've asked for. Watching you overcome your fear will be just as great. Let's get some sweet tea and sit outside. I can gaze off into the wilderness one last time. It's a gorgeous spring day, isn't it?"

"It is, Grandpa, and I love sitting out on the deck."

Kevin and Eddie embrace once again.

Eddie eases into a rocking, laying back and watching the elk graze by the lake. "You know something, Kevin. I'm glad I got to spend this time with you." Eddie takes a long sip of tea and puts down the glass. He closes his eyes, an old pioneer resting for eternity within the endangered frontier.

Kevin's life continues back in New York City amid a societal whirlwind. He occasionally has the bittersweet wish to embrace his grandfather one last time.

One evening Kevin walks home to his apartment while thinking about his grandad. An intruder shoots him just inside his building, steals his wallet, and takes off running. The murderer could not steal the permanent peace of mind that washed over Kevin, who joins Eddie on a ranch that has beauty surpassing the Wyoming vista.

We're on Our Way

Long overdue to leave this rundown city. Work is over for the day. Work is over for the week. It's Independence Day Weekend and summer is in full swing. I'm about to get out of here and enjoy life as it's meant to be enjoyed. I'm packing up with the family and we're moving to Hawaii.

Life is too angry in this urban inferno. Hawaii seems right. Kauai. Kauai is where we're headed. I'm not looking back. We're not looking back. We have plenty of money, family, and opportunities in Hawaii to leave the cosmopolitan worries behind. Packed up and ready to go! A long flight and well worth it. Troubles melt away as the plane reaches new time zones. On the plane, I see the smiles and hopes on the faces of my irresistibly optimistic wife and incredible three children. I thank God he brought them into my life. We're in the sky, never to return to the rundown city we choose to never again call home. A beautiful life awaits in Kauai. We are on our way.

I wake up slowly as my family's happiness and laughter melt away. A family I imagine having as I sleep. Daydreaming at night, within my dreams. I open the blinds in my garden apartment and feel the city noise and litter wash over me. Splashed with the reality that work begins in 30 minutes. The reality that I'm not going to Kauai and I have no family. I do have a garden apartment within which I can dream again tonight, when I might just move my imaginary family to an imaginary place.

A Beautiful Day

Off you go into the cruel world. The only world you've ever known is a world with fear lurking behind every atmospheric phenomenon. You demonize the phenomena and the humans you blame for nature. These humans you ascribe to a permanent class of fallen angels, just as you consider yourself in the permanent class of the gods.

"Hey Mitch! It's a beautiful day out."

"Yeah right, Charmaine. It's so beautiful that it hasn't rained in days."

"What do you mean?"

"I mean it's hot out for this time of year. We really need to stop driving our vehicles."

"But my air conditioning works. Is yours out?"

"I'm not talking about air conditioning. I'm talking about the temperatures. This is unnatural. We have to stop living the way we have been. It's time for a change. A real change. Doesn't it bother you that we're destroying the Earth?"

"I like the Earth and all, but it's not easy to give up my air-conditioned car."

"You don't have to give up driving altogether. Just wait until you can afford an energy efficient vehicle."

"I earn a quarter of a million a year. I think I can afford one now."

"Then why don't you buy one, Charmaine?"

"Aren't you flying on a plane next week, Mitch?"

"Yeah, but I have to travel since I have a real purpose to go where I'm going. You're just driving around for fun."

"Aren't you going to the music festival?"

"Yes, and humanity depends on these festivals as much as it does on saving the Earth from carbon."

"Saving the Earth from carbon? But every day I send email carbon copies. Is that bad?"

"You just don't get it. I sacrifice in other ways, so it's good for me to fly when I need to."

"What sacrifice? You don't have a job."

"Why would I have a job, when that would just contribute to more hurricanes and tornadoes?"

"Hurricanes and tornadoes?

"And blizzards and earthquakes."

"Mitch, where did you get earthquakes from?"

"And meteor showers and planet-destroying asteroids."

"I don't know what you're talking about and I'm not sure you do either."

"Of course you don't. You're a selfish breeder, Charmaine, and you drive a car. I bet you eat animal products, too."

"Are you a vegetarian?"

"No, but I don't want to kill all the animals. If it keeps getting hotter, the Earth will be finished in one year?"

"One year?"

"More like six months."

"Six months?"

"In four weeks for sure."

"That sounds like a bad time, Mitch."

"Only if you live by the water. Ya know, by the oceans."

"But we live by the ocean. How come you're not moving?"

"The flood won't come for me."

"Did you build an ark?"

"What's an ark?"

"Never mind."

"I can't remember a June so hot. Charmaine, by next June it'll be snowing."

"I thought the world was going to disappear by then."

"Not literally. That'll take another year."

"Well then, if everything is going up in flames, I think I'm gonna enjoy the day and grill up some steaks. Care to join me, neighbor? You can just have the macaroni salad if you'd like."

"I don't have to drive over, do I?"

"Seeing as that I'm your next-door neighbor, I don't think you'll need a car."

"That's good, since I don't have one."

"Head on over in an hour."

"You're paying right?"

"I already bought the food."

"That's good, since I don't have any."

"You don't have any money or you don't have any food?"

"Yes."

"See you in an hour."

"Hey Charmaine, would you mind grilling me a steak?"

"No problem. Mitch, I think you'll enjoy it as long as the tragic event doesn't happen first."

"What tragic event?"

"Oh, some neighbor told me a worldwide blizzard or life-ending asteroid is on the way any time now. Haven't you heard?"

THE TALES OF JIMMY ENGLEWOOD (BONUS WRITTEN SERIES)

Jimmy Englewood, Part 1, Crackle

Now 4 AM on October 6th, and Jimmy Englewood senses the autumn winds carry the frequencies of murder. Crackling thunder rocks him out of a deep sleep. Lightning dances frenetically across the sky, matching the brilliance of the storm's decibels.

Jimmy bangs the headboard in disgust over the ongoing string of restless nights. He hits a nerve on the lower right part of his right hand, sending a cascade of slight pain up his arm. Fully awake now, his usually busy mind threatens to keep him up through the sunrise. But this night differs from most. On this night, the rain-doused streets wash away the last vestiges of Jimmy's once thriving hometown.

Rest continues to elude Jimmy. The storm fades into the neighboring suburbs, and the house and sky turn pitch black under the new moon and muted stars. The lamplight next to Jimmy's house on Winston Avenue blows out, as do all the lamplights on his hometown block. Jimmy flicks the light switch on to no avail. No electricity for the night.

Quiet saturates the air on the Avenue, a tree-lined area of town removed from the heart of Marganis. All Jimmy can do is rest his head back on the pillow. Racing thoughts send him in and out of sleep. His heavy eyelids flutter as the morning rays squeeze through the blinds.

The electricity comes back on, though Jimmy would just as soon keep the lights off. He hoists himself up against his will and washes his face. Staring in the mirror, he sees a man holding a gun. Jimmy wrestles the man to the ground. Moments later, the intruder's electricity vanishes for good.

Where Am I?

A piercing ring shatters the silence. The phone volume set on high, Jimmy answers immediately. He regrets answering as a crescendo of fear bolts across his stomach. From the other end of the phone line, the neighbor tells Jimmy, "your brother is dead."

Jimmy loses sight of where he is. The phrase "your brother is dead" paralyzes Jimmy's body and mind. The phrase reverberates in his skull without attenuation. His paralysis quickly melts away and transforms to rage at the words and the deadpan tone on the other end of the line.

"Harold, what the fuck did you just say to me? I've got a dead intruder in my bathroom."

"Jimmy, your brother was murdered. Mary, too. Did you just say you've got a dead intruder in your bathroom?"

Jimmy's heartbeat quickens as he loses his sense of direction. He cannot find a steady rhythm for his breathing. Lightheadedness takes command of his brain.

He imagines Roger's brilliant smile. Roger, Jimmy's younger, now murdered brother, joined in death by Roger's murdered girlfriend, Mary.

Jimmy passes out for a stretch of 30 seconds that feels longer than the lifespan of Heaven. Jimmy is not in Heaven. He cannot pinpoint where he is.

Before the Madness

A brief but penetrating sleep. The 40-year old Jimmy knows he is passed out, and he is aware of Roger's death. But Jimmy wants to enjoy the time travel. While unconscious, he embarks on an odyssey back to memorable times with the brother he loves. If Jimmy can travel back in time, then Roger still lives. Nobody can strip away the memories.

Jimmy and Roger are back home during late summer. A sweltering Friday night, with the aroma of the freshest pizza filling the house. Jimmy 10, and Roger 7, headed to the barbecue up the block the very next day with Mom and Dad at the McElroy's. They couldn't wait to throw the football around and catch up with the McElroy kids.

Hundreds of moments and impressions flash across Jimmy's unconscious. Memories of his parents and friends arise. Memories of his enemies take shape, as do the memories of strangers. Most of all, Jimmy's memories of Roger spring into dreamlike focus.

Jimmy again sees the still image of Roger's smiling face. Time shifts back to the present as Jimmy awakens on the floor, conscious and heartbroken. He knows a funeral and memorial lie in wait. He has not even ventured up the block to Roger's house.

Already dreading the rote feelings of sorrow from family and friends, Jimmy musters the energy to push himself up and walk toward to the living room sliding glass. Blinds already open, Jimmy notices a dash of sunlight as the yellow star disappears behind the clouds and the wind once again picks up. Autumn is here. Jimmy's dreams of times from the past suffer the same fate as Roger and Mary's lives.

The Murders

Jimmy would learn a lot of the details from Harold. Not all of them. Some of the details, neither Harold nor Jimmy could possibly know.

Roger died immediately from the first gunshot. Blasted into the next world without hesitation or guilt. The bullet lodged in the back of his head and scattered fragments of his insides all over the bedroom.

The four gang members scarred Roger's body with 10 shots. From kneecap to elbow, stomach to collarbone, Roger's lifeless body endured damage his mind could no longer sense.

Mary watched the execution as two of the gang members kept watch over her. Stunned by the break in and spirit of wanton violence that crept in the house, she was powerless to move. Wickedness tied her up and bound her in place.

She had looked expressionless at Roger before the gunshot to the back of his head. The wicked spirit already murdered her before the gunshot to her heart, and several more shots into her chest. She felt no pain.

Roger still had life in him during the milliseconds leading up to his murder. He saw the life drawn out of Mary's face as he accepted his destiny to die before the first shot hit him.

The four gang members raised themselves on steady doses of sugary snacks, cheap noodles, and bitter hatreds. Nameless, faceless, and empty. No nuance of decency or minor gradations of evil. They welcomed the full force of evil inside them long ago, and they never let it diminish. They did not organize the two hits, but they carried them out with a degenerate precision and perfection.

Years Ago

During the memorial service for Roger, Jimmy cannot help but think of how dire the situation remains for everyone still alive. After all, the murders become more commonplace by the year. Then by the month. Then by the week...

The neighborhood is now gone. There is no sense of community left. Gone is the notion of societal value and the cherished histories of home, family, and friends. Nothing persists of individual value or individual thought. Everything is over.

Gangs, hucksters, and scavengers patrol the streets. Now a break-in on Winston Avenue does not surprise anybody. The old block limps on in horror as Marganis continues falling apart.

Stone-cold slaughterers just bludgeoned Old lady Canto into a coma. She was the warmest, most gracious woman one could ever meet. The ensconced dregs of society did not administer the beating, as they did to Roger and Mary. Rather, she received her bludgeoning by three of the very many children, now adult males, she used to help, console, and bake cookies for throughout Winston Avenue and the surrounding streets.

Jimmy attends Old Lady Canto's memorial a week after Roger and Mary's funerals. Her murderers stand just outside and stare through the glass of the church. A thorough frost envelopes Jimmy's body in the already damp and dusty dilapidated church.

Not much of a tribute, the shoddy memorial now carries the specter of post-memorial violence. Her murderers are smiling at Jimmy. They forget Jimmy's past kindness to them, just as they forgot Old Lady Canto's when she careened past their punches into a blackout for all time.

Jimmy focuses on Tony and wonders if he and the other two will back off. He wonders whether the weathered and old-timer attendees can help him. They will not, cannot, and do not want to render any aid. Jimmy sees them all leave the church and senses the pain of bruises not yet inflicted. He cannot figure a way out of this house of worship that would not land him in a house of bodily reconstruction.

An anxious Jimmy concentrated so much on getting out of church alive and well, he heard none of the tributes. A great woman died. A woman more caring that he could understand. A woman who Winston Avenue and Marganis discarded long before her death. Jimmy had ignored Old Lady Canto and shunned her to avoid any connection with the old times. He wanted to save his skin, but he now must risk his own skin, muscles, bones, joints, organs, and cartilage to spare his own dwindling independence.

Here they are, the murderers, who urbanites know well as scavengers in the city... Tony and the other two make their presence felt inside the church before Jimmy can muster a plan. His reflexes ice over. The emotional frostbite spreads, and he cannot escape his vulnerability.

Jimmy Englewood, Part 2, Agonizing Epiphany

No luck with Tony. He attacks Jimmy the hardest as the minister becomes the last man to leave Jimmy alone in the room with the scavengers.

The Beating

The sun shines through the cold church floor this early October afternoon. Jimmy never loses consciousness during the thirty-second mugging, and he has all his senses to anticipate and feel every pain, sting, and scratch Tony and his accomplices inflict. No knives or brass knuckles for the scavengers in this assault. They just use bear hands to wail about Jimmy's body and face.

Tony and his lackeys watch with glee as Jimmy stands up and musters a wild punch and connects with Tony's jaw. Stunned for a moment, though unphased in the next, Tony readies his hands for the next stage of the beating.

Jimmy endures a reflexive anguish from his own battered ribs. Nothing broken, but bruises forming everywhere on this hopelessly rebellious shadow of a man.

Tony's accomplices thump to the floor, the first, and then the second. Tony runs as the minister hits him with one of the remaining bullets. Grazed in the arm, Tony keeps running. His accomplices are dead, with one shot a piece enough to riddle both of their backs and render them new inhabitants of the afterworld.

Minister Goshen

Jimmy knows the leadership of Marganis orders beatings as part of the ongoing intimidation campaign. The minister knows it as well, but they both have a bigger problem.

Minister Goshen just killed two men sent by the City Forces.

The City Forces take their orders directly from the city council. The minister, defying the city council and interfering with a recently labeled outcast, Jimmy, must go on the run.

Minister Goshen is too old to run. Not too old in years, but too old in his own skin to try and outsmart the authorities. A man of decency and action, just tidying up his last actions in life. What more can this family man accomplish? His wife and all but one of his four children serve prison sentences for his railing against the banning of large assemblies. His spark remains a motivator to all the continuing holdouts. All the rebels and outcasts see the minister as a father they still have after most of theirs rest in peace, murdered by City Forces and the scavengers.

The minister commands Jimmy to leave. Jimmy, sore from the fresh beating and laboring for oxygen, wants to share his undying gratitude. He cannot find the words. Jimmy stumbles out of the church and back home across the dilapidated church yard and abandoned city parks.

Minister Goshen surveys the two lives he just claimed. Relief washes over him. Not relief for killing two scavengers. Rather, relief for knowing that he took a stand after a series of incidents in which he repeatedly faltered to prolong his own life.

Tony re-emerges at the church, flanked by five armed soldiers of the City Forces. Tony waits at the entrance as the soldiers approach and encircle the minister. They raise their guns in unison toward the minister.

Today there will be no arrests at the church. Some crimes in Marganis must be handled immediately.

This man helped the outcast Jimmy Englewood and defied direct orders from Marganis's leadership. What made him think he'd be allowed to continue his charade of a self-proclaimed free life?

The City Forces left a hand-written message on Jimmy's door that he saw upon arriving home. "The minister is free."

Thus ends the story of Minister Goshen. Jimmy could not attend this memorial service... because there would be no memorial service.

Torment

Everything moves into focus as Jimmy finds the message at his door about the minister. Jimmy survives not by skill or will... not by intelligence or wisdom... not by toughness or usefulness. He survives because the city authorities allow it. He survives because the city authorities encourage it. He survives because the city authorities embrace tormenting chosen victims.

A rebel, yes, yet Jimmy has no power or standing to threaten the authorities. The city leaders hone their abilities to torment as they not only banish Jimmy from society but also banish people from Jimmy's life, and from life itself.

Why choose Jimmy of all people for special torment? He lives as a down-and-out loner and troubled outcast. Jimmy conducts himself as a mere charlatan of a rabble rouser. Still, he is a perfect experimental subject because he has no power. Because he fears isolation. Because the City Forces enjoy feeding people into the spokes of the wheel of hopelessness. If they can drive Jimmy mad, they can drive everyone mad.

Jimmy knows it is only a matter of time before the City Forces change their actions toward him. After the torment, he faces imprisonment or death.

Jimmy has no help in sight. His remaining relatives abandoned him. His old friends would not dare to look in his direction. Nothing remains of his old life. All that's left is his desire to live, an unrelenting purpose the City Forces spend time and effort trying to break.

City Forces

The Marganisan City Council established the City Forces as the law enforcement arm of the Marganis. Formerly the Marganisan Police Department, the reimagined law-enforcement entity morphed into an urban monster. The main purposes of the entity became to smash the will of the disobedient and to get residents to inform on their neighbors. The Council exclaims its will to maintain the democratic integrity of the city at all costs.

Any officers from the old police department became known as soldiers. The City Council declared it so.

The soldiers carried out orders without hesitation. They lost all semblance of mercy and justice for the residents of the city. After confiscating weaponry among many of the residents, the City Forces allowed the gangs and scavengers to keep some of the weaponry to control the people.

Minister Goshen found a way to hide his gun. After the minister killed two of the scavengers, his gun was the last known weapon among the unapproved. The City Forces and City Council feared that many additional weapons could float around in the hands of Marganis's unapproved rebels and outcasts.

Fully Alone

Jimmy walks the empty streets to downtown. Five blocks away. He lives only five blocks away from City Forces Headquarters.

But Jimmy isn't going to City Forces Headquarters. He wants to send the soldiers a message similar to the one they sent him. He wants to send the City Council a message and all of Marganis a message. And so he veers off the straight line to the soldiers' fortress, instead heading directly for the gang members who murdered Roger and Mary. Everyone knows who murdered them.

The Marganisan Enforcers run the criminal underworld throughout the city and beyond. They remain under orders by the City Forces not to brag about it.

But Roger was one of them. He was a member... a high-ranking official in the Marganisan Enforcers. He decided to leave them, and he did, paying for it with his life, and Mary's.

Jimmy walks the empty streets with silent rage. Every mitochondria inside his body cries out to his mind for revenge. He approaches the gang's stronghold, slightly wheezing from the untreated ribs gnawing at his pain receptors.

The minister wasn't the only one with a hidden weapon...

Jimmy walks to the entrance and Tony, the scavenger and friend of the gang, walks out as Jimmy gets ready to knock. A flash of panic deflates Jimmy's stomach. Jimmy draws the handgun from his light jacket and shoots Tony in the solar plexis, just across from Tony's shattered elbow immobilized in a splint. Tony crumples to the floor as the gang members pour outside moments later. Jimmy vanishes through an alley and then hides in plain sight among a gathering crowd heading toward the commotion of Tony's screams. The screams turn to whispering pants as Tony dies.

Before disappearing, Jimmy leaves a hand-written message on the entrance for the Marganisan Enforcers. "Tony is now free."

Jimmy Englewood, Episode 3, They Read Jimmy's Mind

The City Forces knew they were drawing me in to kill somebody. They knew it wouldn't be one of their own. They knew it would be Tony.

Never before, but maybe again

Jimmy never killed anybody. He never even thought of it.

Tony must be dead. He couldn't have suffered a shot like that and lived through it.

The City Forces wanted something over Jimmy, and they wanted Tony gone. Jimmy did not realize it until he slipped into the crowd. Tony was too much of a wildcard. They used him for untold crimes, just as they used the Marganisan Enforcers. The Enforcers are too blinded by rage to know how the City Forces are using them. The City Forces view the enforcers as disposable. The soldiers will continue using the gangs for a while and direct hatred over Tony's death toward Jimmy.

Jimmy has nowhere to go. The Marganisan Enforces or City Forces would hunt him down anywhere in the city. It is merely a matter of hours, if that. Nobody witnessed Jimmy killing Tony, but that would not stop Jimmy from being convicted, with no trial and no jury. If he were to go home now, his life would end.

Minister Goshen's son Derek is close by, living in a modest and concealed home. Nobody knows Jimmy is friends with him. He is the only one who can get Jimmy out of town to escape the impending city bulletins urging the residents to turn Jimmy over to the City Forces.

The nearby towns and unincorporated parts of the broken-up county muddle through, not yet organized enough for the authorities to track Jimmy down. There is too much rebellion outside Marganis for the City Forces or Marganisan Enforcers to catch him. All Derek has to do is get him to the perimeter of the city. Still, Jimmy wonders whether he will have to kill again.

Tony

Tony previously tipped off the gang about when Roger would be home. Roger trusted the wrong people. He thought Tony was his friend. The betrayal enabled the Marganisan Enforcers to murder Jimmy's only brother and Mary.

Jimmy must send a message that he could strike back. Time is not his friend, either inside or outside of the city.

Before Roger joined the gang of Marganisan Enforcers, he meant everything to Jimmy. When Roger left the gang, he rekindled hope in Jimmy to keep living.

Minister Goshen spared Jimmy from harm, physical and spiritual, on more than one occasion. He sacrificed his own life for Jimmy's.

Jimmy now must avenge the deaths of the only people who stood up for him. He did it while sending a message to a city and a movement that despised his very existence.

As Jimmy slips into Derek's house from the alley, he knows without question that Tony is dead. He knows because he has a sinking feeling in crossing a barrier from which he can never return. Jimmy took another man's life and feels overcome with bouts of shame and justification.

Guilt

Derek sees Jimmy enter the side window. Jimmy cannot hide the self-righteous sorrow on his face. He can shake neither the melancholy nor the rationality behind his action. Taking a man's life now seems, at a minimum, remotely acceptable.

Jimmy shot Tony in a fit of purposeful wrath. He combined that rage with cool calculation. At the gang's stronghold, the door opened at just the right time. He did not foresee the timing of taking Tony's life. He just knew he would. Jimmy survived a deadly vengeful escapade, and he knew he would.

The emotions would reach nearly overwhelming heights, from delight to horror to despair to emptiness. Jimmy feels everything, and he feels nothing.

Jimmy's left side tenses up as he feels his ribs screaming for rest. He needs medical attention, but Derek cannot provide that kind of help. Jimmy's eyes shift to the picture on the wall of Derek's dad. Minister Goshen saved Jimmy from being murdered, and Jimmy asks the minister's son to do the same. Fortunately, nobody knows Derek is the minister's son... his illegitimate son from before Minister Goshen devoted his life to his Creator.

Thoughts and impressions flood Jimmy's head. He loses his balance, and Derek breaks his fall before any chance of a concussion.

The city leadership knows everything Jimmy thinks. City Forces anticipate everything he does, and they anticipate perfectly. Jimmy could no longer hide the part of his mind that conceals his objectives from those who mean to destroy him.

Time to leave the city. Any guilt over Tony must wait for a later time. First he has to make sure he can make it out of Derek's house alive, which Jimmy knows is not easy to accomplish when he barely avoids cracking his skull on the hardwood floor. Thanks to Derek, Jimmy's mind is intact. Thanks to the Goshen family, Jimmy is still alive. The pain in his ribs flares up from the sudden jolt as Derek holds Jimmy's limping body. Standing back up is agonizing, but it's yet another moment of suffering to take the fugitive's mind off any remaining guilt.

Jimmy Englewood, Part 4, Fleeing the City

Derek sneaks Jimmy to his car around the corner and drives him out of the city. Just before the City Forces set up a perimeter, Jimmy moves unnoticed across one of the last unguarded zones on the edge of the city. There is no clear video footage on the downtown city streets or buildings... yet. The soldiers, gang members and scavengers cannot muster the manpower or barricades to cover every part of Marganis. Full control over the city lies over the horizon, about a year away.

Trapped on the Run

Jimmy remains trapped out of town... that is, if he ever wants to go back. Going back to Marganis without imprisonment or summary execution would be impossible for this marked criminal. He is an escaped felon in the eyes of Marganisan law.

Jimmy had sent a direct message of defiance before the soldiers could stamp out all the city's nonconformists. He had emboldened the rebels and the marked criminals. The City Forces fear residents could escalate their attacks, ranging from attacks against scavengers and gangsters to attacks against soldiers.

Several miles beyond the outskirts of Marganis, Jimmy feels removed from danger at every step. He walks into a rural zone that has no presence of City Forces, and a weak presence of the gangster Marganisan Enforcers. But scavengers are everywhere. Word spreads about Jimmy killing Tony.

Jimmy walks the rural zone with almost nothing aside from his mind, body, and clothes. His ribs endure great pain. Soldiers and gangsters want him dead. He is lucky to be alive and on the run. Derek is not so fortunate.

Derek

Derek does not drive far enough out of Marganis. He drives Jimmy far enough away from the city, but then he turns back home. As soon as Derek enters Marganis, the City Forces wait for him and surrounded his car. Six armored vehicles close in as Derek sits stunned, knowing his life must now absorb a lot of pain.

In City Forces headquarters, Derek tells them everything. The soldiers know about Jimmy's broken ribs and battered face.

They know Jimmy has Derek's gun and a short supply of food and clothing. They know Derek is the son of Minister Goshen.

After only an hour of questioning, with no violence, fear controls Derek's every sentence... his every word, his every spark of a thought. He no longer exists in a recognizable form. Paralyzed emotions drain the color from his face as he transforms into a craven ghost. His defiance melts away and washes into the lake of spiritual annihilation.

The City Forces transfer Derek to Marganis's ghastly prison. An awe-inspiring building on the outside and an abandoned structure on the inside. A house of daily atrocities fills the prison with rancid sweat, cracked bones, and blackening blood. The building, once a community center, sits atop the old bustling park. The park used to welcome families, couples, and dreamers, enjoying all seasons of city life to replenish themselves in a safe and quiet getaway. The park now hosts dead trees, dead grass, dead spirits, and a prison with a new prisoner. Fallen leaves rustle while rats squirm over the rotting piles.

The price for helping Jimmy is life behind bars. Derek does not have the vigor left to understand what is happening. He enters a permanent trance. It is a trance the soldiers cannot use to their advantage for hard labor or for fighting the nonconformists.

City Forces receive orders from the City Council.

On the fortified and former park grounds, just outside the prison, the soldiers drown Derek in a contaminated fish pond.

Home beyond Reach

Unaware of Derek's fate, Jimmy travels the country landscape into the hazy night. He can never go back willingly to his house, his neighborhood, or his home city. He now faces the perilous specter of his enemies in towns, villages, and cities. Gangsters and scavengers lay in wait to snatch him up for their rewards. They do not own territory outside of Marganis, so Derek has a fighting chance. Yet his fighting chance dwindles by the hour.

The City Council and City Forces grow in power despite the targeted criminals, fugitives, traitors, and nonconformists inside and outside of Marganis. The council and their soldiers have much to improve before seizing power in the old suburban and rural communities. That time threatens to arrive earlier than twelve moons from now. The Marganisan leaders already have the power to block a man from returning to his home or from returning to his normal life.

Jimmy imagines the soldiers destroying his home... more of a vision than an imagining. The soldiers steal any remaining valuables in Jimmy's house before blowing it up with dynamite.

Never again can Jimmy get back to his home. He has no place of solace and refuge to keep the monsters of the past and present at bay.

Congealed fog dampens the starlight as the temperatures plummet. Heat escapes Jimmy's exhausted body. His mind ignores his broken bones amidst a ravenous hunger and insatiable desire for sleep. Jimmy keeps moving through the farmlands and fields until he peers through heavy eyelids to see the great palatial estate of his magical memories. The fog breaks momentarily and he lumbers toward the estate with purposeful abandon. An unsuspecting Jimmy is about to face his longtime nightmares. A bellowing howl reverberates across the large expanse of property. A husky jumps through the low-lying damp clouds to greet Jimmy at the gate.

Jimmy's thoughts of his house disappear. His very idea of a home transfers to this grand estate outside Marganis. As Jimmy soon observes, any notion of a physical home lies beyond his reality. The husky smiles and welcomes the long-lost visitor.

To be continued

ACKNOWLEDGEMENTS

I thank God, with whom everything is possible. I am grateful to my family and friends for their outstanding support. And to my cousin Eddie, gone but not forgotten. Thank you to all my readers.

ABOUT THE AUTHOR

Author Jeremy Gravilore creates for audiences seeking raw stories. From speculative fiction to vignettes, the mid-Atlantic native writes evocative poetry and thought-provoking prose. Jeremy's storytelling inspiration stretches across radio, movies, television, live theater, and music. A Gen Xer with an ancient soul, he finds creative influences ranging from the ***Bible*** to ***The Odyssey***, ***1984*** to ***Lord of the Flies***, ***The Twilight Zone*** to ***Columbo***, and ***Abbott and Costello Meet Frankenstein*** to ***Blade Runner***. Jeremy enjoys traveling around America. He loves the natural world, but it is his love for captivating stories of the mind, soul, and civilization that motivates him to construct old worlds and new.

9 781962 768054